T0015868

200 Prayers for a POSITIVE MINDSET

VALORIE QUESENBERRY

200 Prayers for a POSITIVE MINDSET

BARBOUR
PUBLISHING

© 2022 by Barbour Publishing, Inc

Print ISBN 978-1-63609-380-2

All rights reserved. No part of this publication may be reproduced or transmitted for commercial purposes, except for brief quotations in printed reviews, without written permission of the publisher. Reproduced text may not be used on the World Wide Web.

Churches and other noncommercial interests may reproduce portions of this book without the express written permission of Barbour Publishing, provided that the text does not exceed 500 words or 5 percent of the entire book, whichever is less, and that the text is not from material quoted from another publisher. When reproducing text from this book, include the following credit line: "From *200 Prayers for a Positive Mindset*, published by Barbour Publishing, Inc. Used by permission."

Scripture quotations marked NKJV are taken from the New King James Version®. Copyright © 1982 by Thomas Nelson, Inc. Used by permission. All rights reserved.

Scripture quotations marked ESV are from The Holy Bible, English Standard Version®. Text Edition: 2016. Copyright © 2001 by Crossway, a publishing ministry of Good News Publishers. The ESV® text has been reproduced in cooperation with and by permission of Good News Publishers. Unauthorized reproduction of this publication is prohibited. All rights reserved.

Scripture quotations marked AMPC are taken from the Amplified® Bible, Classic Edition, Copyright © 1954, 1958, 1962, 1964, 1965, 1987 by The Lockman Foundation. Used by permission.

Scripture quotations marked PHILLIPS are taken from The New Testament in Modern English by J. B. Phillips copyright © 1960, 1972 J. B. Phillips. Administered by The Archbishops' Council of the Church of England. Used by permission.

Scripture quotation marked KJV is taken from the King James Version of the Bible.

Published by Barbour Publishing, Inc., 1810 Barbour Drive, Uhrichsville, Ohio 44683, www.barbourbooks.com

Our mission is to inspire the world with the life-changing message of the Bible.

Member of the
Evangelical Christian
Publishers Association

Printed in China.

A Mind Set on Purpose

YOUR MARK ON ME

To the intent that now the manifold wisdom of God might be made known by the church to the principalities and powers in the heavenly places, according to the eternal purpose which he accomplished in Christ Jesus our Lord, in whom we have boldness and access with confidence through faith in Him.

EPHESIANS 3:10–12 NKJV

Heavenly Father, as I start this new day, I rejoice in the purpose You have for me. Thank You for choosing me to be Your daughter. Long before I was born, You put Your eternal mark on my soul and planned for me to be redeemed by Your love. As a little girl, I longed for love and beauty and safety. And I found out that only in You could I really find all these things. The friendships and relationships I had were sweet for a time, but eventually they reached a point where they could not fulfill me. Thank You for using Your Word and Your family to point me in the right direction. I don't have to live a life of meaningless days and empty nights. You are the source and center of my fulfillment. Your mark on me doesn't mean that nothing goes wrong but that You are with me through it all. I love You, Father. Amen.

MY CALL

And we know that all things work together for good to those who love God, to those who are the called according to His purpose. For whom He foreknew, He also predestined to be conformed to the image of His Son, that He might be the firstborn among many brethren. Moreover whom He predestined, these He also called; whom He called, these He also justified; and whom He justified, these He also glorified. What then shall we say to these things? If God is for us, who can be against us?

ROMANS 8:28–31 NKJV

. . . .

Dear Father, so many things around me pull me away from the purpose You have for me. But I know that You made me for a reason, and You are working to fulfill that purpose as I continually surrender to You. Not everything that happens to me *is* good. This world is fallen and imperfect; others are sinful and unloving. But everything that happens to me as Your daughter is part of a weaving of good that You are completing. You can redeem whatever happens to me for Your purpose. And since You are for me, who can be against me? Amen!

GENEROUS PURPOSES

So let each one give as he purposes in his heart, not grudgingly or of necessity; for God loves a cheerful giver. And God is able to make all grace abound toward you, that you, always having all sufficiency in all things, may have an abundance for every good work. As it is written: "He has dispersed abroad, He has given to the poor; His righteousness endures forever."

2 CORINTHIANS 9:7–9 NKJV

Lord, today I don't feel like being cheerful, nor do I feel in a particularly giving mood; but You've said that You love a giver who is cheerful, so I will do my best to give cheerfully. The principle of cheerful giving applies not only to whatever money or assets I have but also to my time and my talents and my encouragement of others. Often it can be easy to give superficial care to others, but You call us to be genuine and to offer our love and compassion in generous ways. I want Your grace to abound toward me, so today I purpose in my heart to give to others as You have given to me. Amen.

MY SEASON OF PURPOSE

To everything there is a season, a time for every purpose under heaven: a time to be born, and a time to die; a time to plant, and a time to pluck what is planted; a time to kill, and a time to heal; a time to break down, and a time to build up; a time to weep, and a time to laugh; a time to mourn, and a time to dance.

ECCLESIASTES 3:1–4 NKJV

Lord God, I rejoice today in Your purposes and seasons. To my way of thinking, the times and seasons run together, year after year, each one seeming to go by faster than the previous one. But from Your perspective, the seasons keep a steady beat, accomplishing what You desire in me as I surrender to Your will.

I don't like the dying times, the plucking times, or the weeping and mourning times. But in Your hand, they are as necessary as being born and planting and laughing and dancing. They are part of the pattern You are using to grow me to reflect You. I submit to Your seasons today. Amen.

PURPOSE IN MY SUFFERING

Share with me in the sufferings for the gospel according to the power of God, who has saved us and called us with a holy calling, not according to our works, but according to His own purpose and grace which was given to us in Christ Jesus before time began, but has now been revealed by the appearing of our Savior Jesus Christ, who has abolished death and brought life and immortality to light through the gospel.

2 TIMOTHY 1:8–10 NKJV

Father God, when I was little, I didn't understand that suffering was a normal part of life. I thought that getting hurt was unusual and that my mom should be there to make things better. But as I've grown older, I've come to realize that getting hurt is to be expected in this life. The roses do have thorns, and the clouds do hold rain; people and pets and projects can become sources of pain.

That's why I'm so glad that Your Son, Jesus, destroyed death and brought eternal life! And my pain today has a purpose, because everything You allow is part of the glory yet to come. I rest my soul in that truth! Amen.

SET APART AND STILL

But know that the LORD has set apart for Himself him
who is godly; the LORD will hear when I call to Him.
Be angry, and do not sin. Meditate within your heart
on your bed, and be still Selah. Offer the sacrifices
of righteousness, and put your trust in the LORD.

PSALM 4:3–5 NKJV

. . . .

Dear Father in heaven, Your Word is truth, and today I see myself in it. I am tempted to be angry when I call out to You and it seems You aren't listening. I forget that You have set me apart to be holy and righteous. Too often I think You should operate on my terms and within my time frame. But You tell me to meditate on You while I lie in bed, and not to stare into the night thinking bitter thoughts. Show me how to offer the sacrifices of righteousness and to trust You, no matter what is going on in the world around me. Each night as I go to sleep, help me to be reflecting on You and Your goodness. I ask this in Jesus' name. Amen.

THE SET OF MY EYES

The Lord is my chosen and assigned portion, my cup;
You hold and maintain my lot. The lines have fallen
for me in pleasant places; yes, I have a good heritage.
I will bless the Lord, Who has given me counsel; yes,
my heart instructs me in the night seasons. I have
set the Lord continually before me; because He is at
my right hand, I shall not be moved. Therefore my
heart is glad and my glory [my inner self] rejoices; my
body too shall rest and confidently dwell in safety.

PSALM 16:5-9 AMPC

Lord God, nothing is hidden from You. You can see all the intentions of my heart. The culture around me tells me to follow my heart, but You tell me to surrender my heart to Your purpose and set it on You. Just like the psalmist, I am holding You out before me as my salvation and highest joy. Fixing my eyes on You gives me both physical rest and spiritual rest. I feel secure when I know I am following the right way—Your way. I bless Your name today. Amen.

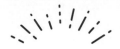

THE SOURCE OF MY SECURITY

Yes, You are my Rock and my Fortress;
therefore for Your name's sake lead me and guide
me. Draw me out of the net that they have laid
secretly for me, for You are my Strength and my
Stronghold. Into Your hands I commit my spirit; You
have redeemed me, O Lord, the God of truth and
faithfulness. [You and] I abhor those who pay regard to
vain idols; but I trust in, rely on, and confidently lean on
the Lord. I will be glad and rejoice in Your mercy and
steadfast love, because You have seen my affliction,
You have taken note of my life's distresses, and You
have not given me into the hand of the enemy;
You have set my feet in a broad place.

PSALM 31:3–8 AMPC

. . . .

Father in heaven, today I proclaim that You are my Rock
and Fortress. I have no strength without You to face this
life I live. You have created me and redeemed me, and I
trust my soul to You. As I go through my days, interacting
with others, dealing with disappointments, and serving my
family, I'm sometimes tempted to be discouraged. I feel
hemmed in by the obligations and stresses of life. But I
know You have set my spiritual feet in a broad place, and
I will not be moved. Amen.

PURPOSEFUL INTEGRITY

I will sing of steadfast love and justice; to you, O LORD, I will make music. I will ponder the way that is blameless. Oh when will you come to me? I will walk with integrity of heart within my house; I will not set before my eyes anything that is worthless.

PSALM 101:1–3 ESV

. . . .

Dear Lord, there have been times in my life when I viewed worthless things, when I valued worthless things. I realize now how wrong that was. I am so glad to know the truth. Lord, the only things worth valuing are Your steadfast love and justice. You want me to be blameless in my actions, to choose integrity and not evil.

Today, Lord, my mind is set on discovering Your will in everything I do. I believe Your Word addresses all the themes that are important to life. You have given us instruction in every facet of living. Instead of learning what to value from a screen reflecting earthly wisdom, I choose to learn from You. Amen.

BOUNDARY SETTER

*He set the earth on its foundations, so that it should
never be moved. You covered it with the deep as with
a garment; the waters stood above the mountains.
At your rebuke they fled; at the sound of your thunder
they took to flight. The mountains rose, the valleys
sank down to the place that you appointed for
them. You set a boundary that they may not pass,
so that they might not again cover the earth.*

PSALM 104:5–9 ESV

• •

Dear God, when I look at the complications in my life, they
resemble floodwaters rising all around me, threatening
my security and serenity. How easily I forget that Jesus
calmed the storm with words of rebuke. Instead I feel close
to drowning under my troubles, all alone and forgotten.
The disciples must have felt that way in their little boat
before they woke Jesus from His slumber in the stern.

And yet the psalmist reminds me that, to You, the
oceans of the earth are like a pretty garment that You
spread over the place You desire. You set the boundaries
for their tides. Today I ask You to keep my head above
the water, and I trust You to do it. Amen.

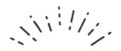

PURPOSED FOR TRIUMPH

For the righteous will never be moved; he will
be remembered forever. He is not afraid of
bad news; his heart is firm, trusting in the LORD.
His heart is steady; he will not be afraid, until
he looks in triumph on his adversaries.

PSALM 112:6–8 ESV

• •

Heavenly Father, no bad news on this earth is greater than Your power to keep me steady. I think of those in the Bible who received bad news; Job especially comes to mind. He lost his children, his home, his possessions, and his land in one afternoon, and yet You kept his heart firm, trusting in the Lord.

I know that You have purposed me to triumph over my adversity. That doesn't mean I won't feel the grief of loss, but it does mean that I won't be moved from Your plan for me if I look to You for direction—whatever happens around me. Thank You for the grace You've promised to keep me going. Amen.

BORDERED BY PROVIDENCE

O Lord, you have searched me and known me! You know when I sit down and when I rise up; you discern my thoughts from afar. You search out my path and my lying down and are acquainted with all my ways. Even before a word is on my tongue, behold, O Lord, you know it altogether. You hem me in, behind and before, and lay your hand upon me. Such knowledge is too wonderful for me; it is high; I cannot attain it.

PSALM 139:1–6 ESV

God Almighty, You alone are the One who knows all my thoughts and intentions. You see my actions before I do them. You know what keeps me awake at night and what makes me laugh. You have prior knowledge of the things that will happen in my life today. You are intimately aware of the happenings of my day, even down to my bedtime and the number of times I hit the snooze button. Like the psalmist David, I can say that You have hemmed me in, put me in a place where You are all around me. That thought comforts me now that I know You as my Savior. I rest in the fact that You know everything about me. Amen.

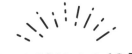

PURPOSEFUL WORDS

O Lord, I call upon you; hasten to me! Give ear to my voice when I call to you! Let my prayer be counted as incense before you, and the lifting up of my hands as the evening sacrifice! Set a guard, O Lord, over my mouth; keep watch over the door of my lips!

PSALM 141:1–3 ESV

. . . .

O Lord, it's morning. My alarm awakened me before I was ready. Why is it that I have trouble falling asleep at night, yet I have trouble waking up in the morning? I wonder... when You walked the earth, did You experience this too?

Now it's time for me to face my day. And I know I need Your discernment and control as I use words today. If I were a prophet on a hillside, I would lift my hands to You as the fragrance from my sacrifice rose toward the heavens. Since I'm alone in my room, I will still lift my hands and ask You to keep the words of my mouth the way a palace guard stands watch beside the entrance. May no unwholesome or unloving words escape that watch today! In Jesus' name. Amen.

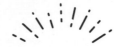

ESTABLISHED FOR A PURPOSE

When the tempest passes, the wicked is no more,
but the righteous is established forever. . . . The fear
of the LORD prolongs life, but the years of the wicked
will be short. The hope of the righteous brings joy,
but the expectation of the wicked will perish. The
way of the LORD is a stronghold to the blameless.

PROVERBS 10:25, 27–29 ESV

Father in heaven, You have planned that I would be established forever. That is something I find difficult to comprehend. Everything around me is built on temporary sentiment—fashion, fads, technology, architecture, and business—all of it gains traction based on the whims of society and a few movers and shakers who influence the rest of us. But You operate in the realm of eternity where things are settled according to a different measure. You say that those who practice wickedness will have a short existence, and I know that refers to their tiny bit of life here on earth. But the righteous will be established forever, and that means eternal life with You. You are a stronghold for me today. Amen.

A FIXED HEART

*My heart is fixed, O God, my heart is steadfast
and confident! I will sing and make melody. Awake,
my glory (my inner self); awake, harp and lyre! I
will awake right early [I will awaken the dawn]! I will
praise and give thanks to You, O Lord, among the
peoples; I will sing praises to You among the nations.
For Your mercy and loving-kindness are great,
reaching to the heavens, and Your truth and
faithfulness to the clouds. Be exalted, O God, above
the heavens; let Your glory be over all the earth.*

PSALM 57:7–11 AMPC

. . . .

O God, Your heavens are high above us all, and Your
truth and faithfulness reach to the clouds. Your purpose
for this earth and its inhabitants is good; I want to be part
of it. You are exalted and praised by the hosts of heaven,
and I will give praise to You too. I want to lift my song to
You with the dawn. I am singing in my inner self to You
right now, even as I'm doing all the other things that life
requires of me. I recognize that only living for You gives
me a reason to keep going. My heart is fixed and settled
in this purpose. In Jesus' name. Amen.

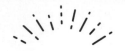

UNSHAKEN PURPOSE

*A good man deals graciously and lends; he will
guide his affairs with discretion. Surely he will
never be shaken; the righteous will be in everlasting
remembrance. He will not be afraid of evil tidings;
his heart is steadfast, trusting in the LORD. His
heart is established; he will not be afraid,
until he sees his desire upon his enemies.*

PSALM 112:5–8 NKJV

Dear Lord, I want my heart to be established in You.
So many things frighten me, but Your Word says that I
don't have to fear when I hear about all the bad things
happening around me. The purpose of my life is so firmly
rooted in You that I can remain centered and steadfast,
trusting You for my future.

Lord, all around me people are shaken—my unsaved
family members, my coworkers, my acquaintances in the
community, the people I pass as I go about my day. But
today I set my heart on You, so that You can work out Your
unshaken purpose in and through me. I have confidence
that today is going to be a good day because You hold it
in Your hands. Amen.

A Mind Set on Purity

MADE PURE BY THE WORD

The law of the LORD is perfect, reviving the soul; the testimony of the LORD is sure, making wise the simple; the precepts of the LORD are right, rejoicing the heart; the commandment of the LORD is pure, enlightening the eyes; the fear of the LORD is clean, enduring forever; the rules of the LORD are true, and righteous altogether. More to be desired are they than gold, even much fine gold; sweeter also than honey and drippings of the honeycomb. Moreover, by them is your servant warned; in keeping them there is great reward.

PSALM 19:7–11 ESV

O Lord, You are supremely righteous. And everything You do is righteous. That means that the Word You gave us is fully true and perfect, lacking nothing. When I read it, I am revived and made wise; my heart rejoices, and my vision is made clear. As I develop an appetite for the Bible, I find that it is sweetness to my soul. What's more, it warns me of dangers. Thank You for the reward to be found in regularly spending time in this great treasure— it helps me keep my mind set on purity. And nothing is more positive than that! Amen.

DAYS FILLED WITH PURE DEEDS

Who shall ascend the hill of the LORD? And who shall stand in his holy place? He who has clean hands and a pure heart, who does not lift up his soul to what is false and does not swear deceitfully. He will receive blessing from the LORD and righteousness from the God of his salvation.

PSALM 24:3–5 ESV

. . . .

Lord God, You dwell in absolute holiness. You are the essence of absolute holiness. Nothing that is stained or soiled can come near You; the brightness of Your presence would annihilate it. That's why You want to make me holy through the shed blood of Jesus. Because of His sacrifice, I can be clean. And that means that both my hands (my actions) and my heart (my motives) can be pure in Your sight. The only way I can receive Your blessing is if I let Your Spirit cleanse me until I sparkle from the inside out. Please start that process today! Amen.

PURE WORDS

*The words of the LORD are pure words, like silver
tried in a furnace of earth, purified seven times.
You shall keep them, O LORD, You shall preserve
them from this generation forever.*

PSALM 12:6–7 NKJV

. . . .

Dear Lord, when I first get up in the morning, I'm hungry—
hungry for food for my body. And yet, as I spend more
time in Your Word, I find I'm also hungry for the nourishment of truth. The Bible is Your truth, pure words, preserved for me to read so that I can know how to live. Lord,
the world around me knows nothing of the delight I find
in reading what You inspired the prophets and other
Bible writers to record thousands of years ago. But You
have allowed me to find that joy, and today I thank You for
protecting Your truth for all the ones like me who depend
on it for strength to live. Thank You for every person out
there who gives out Bibles to others. May they come to
relish its sustenance like I do. Amen.

PURITY IS THE PASSWORD

"Blessed are the poor in spirit, for theirs is the kingdom of heaven. Blessed are those who mourn, for they shall be comforted. Blessed are the meek, for they shall inherit the earth. Blessed are those who hunger and thirst for righteousness, for they shall be satisfied. Blessed are the merciful, for they shall receive mercy. Blessed are the pure in heart, for they shall see God. Blessed are the peacemakers, for they shall be called sons of God."

MATTHEW 5:3–9 ESV

God in heaven, here on earth, purity isn't valued very much unless it refers to being free of disease or infection. Certainly, the idea of being pure in heart is not on most people's radar. Purity means being wholly pure. Most people in our culture expect to have a little greed and deception and selfishness operating in their motives. But You, Lord, call us and enable us to have a purity that begins in the spirit and then plays out in our actions. Your Word says this purity is a prerequisite for seeing You face-to-face. I ask You to work Your purity in me as I surrender my will to Yours. In Jesus' name. Amen.

SET APART FOR GOD'S USE

But God's firm foundation stands, bearing this seal:
"The Lord knows those who are his," and, "Let everyone
who names the name of the Lord depart from iniquity."
... Therefore, if anyone cleanses himself from what is
dishonorable, he will be a vessel for honorable use,
set apart as holy, useful to the master of the house,
ready for every good work. So flee youthful passions
and pursue righteousness, faith, love, and peace, along
with those who call on the Lord from a pure heart.

2 TIMOTHY 2:19, 21–22 ESV

O Lord, today I want to be set apart and reserved for Your particular use. I want the focus of my life to be doing Your will, because living for You and Your glory is the key to fulfillment. And in order to be used by You, I must be sanctified and cleansed so that I can walk in step with Your Holy Spirit. Only then will I experience true joy in my life. No mindset is more positive than one of knowing that I'm walking in fellowship with the God of the universe. Today, please work out Your perfect purpose in me. In Jesus' name. Amen.

CONFIDENCE THROUGH PURITY

Therefore, brothers, since we have confidence to enter the holy places by the blood of Jesus, by the new and living way that he opened for us through the curtain, that is, through his flesh, and since we have a great priest over the house of God, let us draw near with a true heart in full assurance of faith, with our hearts sprinkled clean from an evil conscience and our bodies washed with pure water. Let us hold fast the confession of our hope without wavering, for he who promised is faithful. And let us consider how to stir up one another to love and good works.

HEBREWS 10:19–24 ESV

Dear Lord, confidence is an attractive trait. And it can be challenging to acquire if one is not naturally full of bravado or a great actor. True confidence requires that I rest in an attitude of security, and often I don't feel very secure. But I'm discovering that I can have confidence when I hold fast to Your promises and trust You for strength to do what needs to be done. You are faithful, and You have promised never to leave me or forsake me as I live in Your light. Amen.

PURE RELIGION MAKES ME A SERVANT

But the one who looks into the perfect law, the law of liberty, and perseveres, being no hearer who forgets but a doer who acts, he will be blessed in his doing. If anyone thinks he is religious and does not bridle his tongue but deceives his heart, this person's religion is worthless. Religion that is pure and undefiled before God the Father is this: to visit orphans and widows in their affliction, and to keep oneself unstained from the world.

JAMES 1:25–27 ESV

• •

Lord, I hear a lot about being a servant. And I want to be. But I have found that my actions always follow my beliefs. That's why the idea of believing in order to be saved is so powerful. True belief changes the actions and verifies that something good is operating deep within. I can't be a servant to others unless You have changed me on the inside. And then I can have a way of following Christ, a religion, that is not stuffy or arrogant or confused but rather borne out in righteous actions for the good of others and in an attitude that guards my inner life against the depravity of the godless culture. Amen.

PURE WISDOM

*But if you have bitter jealousy and selfish ambition
in your hearts, do not boast and be false to the truth.
This is not the wisdom that comes down from above,
but is earthly, unspiritual, demonic. For where jealousy
and selfish ambition exist, there will be disorder
and every vile practice. But the wisdom from above
is first pure, then peaceable, gentle, open to reason,
full of mercy and good fruits, impartial and sincere.
And a harvest of righteousness is sown in
peace by those who make peace.*

JAMES 3:14–18 ESV

. . . .

Lord, as long as I depend on the world's wisdom, I will live my life according to the wrong set of ideals. The wisdom of this age is self-serving and open to evil practices that dishonor You. The wisdom of the current culture says that truth is relative and there are no clear lines around what is right for everyone. But You are the embodiment of truth, and to know You is to walk in clarity and true wisdom. This wisdom is first pure and holy; it does not blaspheme You nor take advantage of others. It manifests itself in noble and just attitudes and actions. And it brings a harvest of righteousness. This is the best mindset I can have today. Amen.

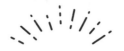

OBEDIENCE AND PURITY

Since you have purified your souls in obeying the truth through the Spirit in sincere love of the brethren, love one another fervently with a pure heart, having been born again, not of corruptible seed but incorruptible, through the word of God which lives and abides forever, because "All flesh is as grass, and all the glory of man as the flower of the grass. The grass withers, and its flower falls away, but the word of the LORD endures forever." Now this is the word which by the gospel was preached to you.

1 PETER 1:22–25 NKJV

O God, I thank You today for Your Word, which doesn't fade or wither; it is ever living. Because of its truth, I can know how to follow You and love others. This is the heart of purity.

When Jesus was on earth, He was asked what was the greatest commandment. And He answered, "'You shall love the LORD your God with all your heart, with all your soul, and with all your mind.' . . . And the second is like it: 'You shall love your neighbor as yourself'" (Matthew 22:37, 39 NKJV). Keeping this command is what real holy living is all about. And that is what gives me a positive mindset today—knowing I am obeying You, as I purpose to love You and others. Amen.

PURE HOPE MAKES ME HAPPY

*Behold what manner of love the Father has bestowed
on us, that we should be called children of God! Therefore
the world does not know us, because it did not know
Him. Beloved, now we are children of God; and it
has not yet been revealed what we shall be, but we
know that when He is revealed, we shall be like Him,
for we shall see Him as He is. And everyone who has
this hope in Him purifies himself, just as He is pure.*

1 JOHN 3:1–3 NKJV

Father God, no joy compares to the joy of anticipating
something wonderful! When I was a little girl, even small
things could make me excited—a new toy, a trip, a treat.
Now that I'm older, I don't get so gushy about things to
come. I've had some big disappointments in life. Some
things that I thought would come to pass—that I really
wanted to come to pass—didn't. That's why I want to
take hold of the joy of these verses today and get excited
about them. There is pure happiness in the fact that
someday, because I have trusted in You for salvation,
I will see You and be made like You. Thank You for this
magnificent joy to come. Amen!

A PURE CITY FOR US

Now the wall of the city had twelve foundations, and on them were the names of the twelve apostles of the Lamb.... The construction of its wall was of jasper; and the city was pure gold, like clear glass. The foundations of the wall of the city were adorned with all kinds of precious stones.... The twelve gates were twelve pearls: each individual gate was of one pearl. And the street of the city was pure gold, like transparent glass.

REVELATION 21:14, 18–19, 21 NKJV

Holy Lord, You are the great Creator. Everything You design is perfection. The curse of sin has marred Your creation, but You have redeemed our souls through the sacrifice of Jesus; and someday You will redeem our bodies and create a new heaven and earth. That place will be the purest residence we've ever had. Your Word says it is a city of pure gold.

Lord, I'm so glad You can make me ready to inhabit this city. No sin will enter there. Neither will disease or infection or any kind of corruption. I look ahead with delight to living in a city that will never need to be reclaimed. It is eternally holy and good, full of joy and peace. Thank You! Amen.

PURE PLEASURE FOR ETERNITY

And he showed me a pure river of water of life, clear as crystal, proceeding from the throne of God and of the Lamb. In the middle of its street, and on either side of the river, was the tree of life, which bore twelve fruits, each tree yielding its fruit every month. The leaves of the tree were for the healing of the nations. And there shall be no more curse, but the throne of God and of the Lamb shall be in it, and His servants shall serve Him. They shall see His face, and His name shall be on their foreheads. There shall be no night there: They need no lamp nor light of the sun, for the Lord God gives them light. And they shall reign forever and ever.

REVELATION 22:1–5 NKJV

God my Father, I feel blessed to read these words and imagine what it will be like to live in Your perfect home. The river is pure, life-giving water because it comes from You. There is no curse on the land, and You dwell there with Your people. You will be the light—always on, always bright, never flickering or experiencing a power shortage. Lord, the place You have prepared for Your people sounds amazing, and keeping that promise alive in me gives me strength to face each new day. Amen!

A Mind Set on Plain Speech

OBEDIENCE TO GOD'S COMMANDS

*"These are the statutes and judgments which you shall
be careful to observe in the land which the LORD God
of your fathers is giving you to possess, all the days
that you live on the earth.... Observe and obey all
these words which I command you, that it may go well
with you and your children after you forever, when
you do what is good and right in the sight of the LORD
your God.... Whatever I command you, be careful to
observe it; you shall not add to it nor take away from it."*

DEUTERONOMY 12:1, 28, 32 NKJV

Dear God, after You delivered Your people from Egypt,
You gave them very specific directions about how to live
for Your glory. And it was very important for them to follow
the commands You gave them. Today, Lord, there are those
who say that a relationship with You is all freedom and no
rules. But I know that isn't true. You are the same in every
generation; and if You cared about boundaries long ago,
You care about them today too. Thank You for giving me
security by communicating with me through Your Word.
Help me to obey Your commands. Amen.

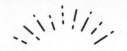

WORDS OF BLESSING

"So let Your name be magnified forever, saying, 'The LORD of hosts is the God over Israel.'... And now, O Lord GOD, You are God, and Your words are true, and You have promised this goodness to Your servant. Now therefore, let it please You to bless the house of Your servant, that it may continue before You forever; for You, O Lord GOD, have spoken it, and with Your blessing let the house of Your servant be blessed forever."

2 SAMUEL 7:26, 28–29 NKJV

• •

Lord God, I am blessed by the words You give others. Generations ago, You inspired the Bible writers; they were under Your anointing and power. The words they painstakingly and reverently preserved are Yours—life-giving, holy, instructive, comforting, and faith-building. Thank You for the Bible.

In my life, others have spoken words that have challenged and motivated and encouraged me. It's not the same as the way You inspired the Bible, but still You give good men and women the thoughts that they share with others. I've been the receiver of such words of blessing, and I'm so grateful You've used others to bless me in this way.

WORDS THAT BRING CONVICTION AND CHANGE

Then Shaphan the scribe told the king, saying, "Hilkiah the priest has given me a book." And Shaphan read it before the king. Thus it happened, when the king heard the words of the Law, that he tore his clothes. Then the king commanded. . ."Go, inquire of the LORD for me, and for those who are left in Israel and Judah, concerning the words of the book that is found; for great is the wrath of the LORD that is poured out on us, because our fathers have not kept the word of the LORD, to do according to all that is written in this book."

2 CHRONICLES 34:18–21 NKJV

. . . .

Dear Father, You have given us the gift of language, and we use it to communicate with You and with each other. You speak the languages of the nations and see all the way to the hearts of the speakers—where their words originate. When we do wrong, You have chosen to use words to convict us and point us back to truth. I'm so glad You showed me the way back to You through the death of Jesus. And You have used words to tell me about it. I'm grateful. Amen.

WORDS OF COVENANT

*And he read in their hearing all the words of the Book
of the Covenant which had been found in the house of
the LORD. Then the king stood in his place and made a
covenant before the LORD, to follow the LORD, and to
keep His commandments and His testimonies and His
statutes with all his heart and all his soul, to perform the
words of the covenant that were written in this book.*

2 CHRONICLES 34:30–31 NKJV

Dear Lord, promises are often broken in the realm where
I live. Spouses promise to stay together but don't; politicians promise to make changes but don't; corporations
and institutions promise to live up to their signed agreements, but don't. It's frustrating to live in a place where
so many things don't last.

The king in this passage from 2 Chronicles was
determined to make a covenant and keep it. He decided
to perform the words he heard in the Book. His action
gives me inspiration. In a culture where things don't last,
my commitment to You can.

Today, Lord Jesus, when I am tempted to put a low
value on the things of eternity, remind me of the covenant
I have made to follow You. Amen.

CONVERSING WITH THE ALMIGHTY

"How then can I answer Him, and choose my words to reason with Him? For though I were righteous, I could not answer Him; I would beg mercy of my Judge. If I called and He answered me, I would not believe that He was listening to my voice. For He crushes me with a tempest, and multiplies my wounds without cause. He will not allow me to catch my breath, but fills me with bitterness. If it is a matter of strength, indeed He is strong; and if of justice, who will appoint my day in court? Though I were righteous, my own mouth would condemn me; though I were blameless, it would prove me perverse.

JOB 9:14–20 NKJV

Lord God, when I'm tempted to lash out at You and question Your way of doing things, when I feel that I have acquired so much wisdom, when I get too full of myself . . .remind me of these words from the story of Job. He suffered much more than I ever have, and he wanted to understand all that was going on. But there was no way he could. We don't need to debate You but need only to trust You. You are perfectly holy, and so You can never be anything but perfectly good toward us. Amen.

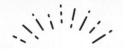

WORDS THAT PRESERVE

Help, LORD, for the godly man ceases! For the faithful disappear from among the sons of men. They speak idly everyone with his neighbor; with flattering lips and a double heart they speak. May the LORD cut off all flattering lips, and the tongue that speaks proud things. . . . The words of the LORD are pure words, like silver tried in a furnace of earth, purified seven times. You shall keep them, O LORD, You shall preserve them from this generation forever.

PSALM 12:1–3, 6–7 NKJV

Lord God, words of flattery and vanity soon spoil. They are tainted from the inside out. Words of deception have the principle of death at work in them. They cannot last, for they are not true. But the words You speak are pure like silver tested in a smelting furnace. They are without residue, clean and crystal clear through and through. These words are faithful, and they will preserve me. So today, Lord, I ask You to lift my eyes to Your words. They last forever. Amen.

THE PLAIN SPEECH
OF THE HEAVENS

*The heavens declare the glory of God; and the
firmament shows His handiwork. Day unto day utters
speech, and night unto night reveals knowledge.
There is no speech nor language where their voice
is not heard. Their line has gone out through all
the earth, and their words to the end of the world.
In them He has set a tabernacle for the sun.*

PSALM 19:1–4 NKJV

Creator God, no words could be plainer to read than
the ones written in the skies. These verses tell me that
You have put language into the universe, a language that
communicates Your character and Your good purposes
for us.

Sometimes I misunderstand what others say, especially
those with whom I communicate a lot. Even living in the
same house doesn't mean we'll always fully understand
what someone is saying. And then we might become
irritated with one another, making communication even
more difficult.

I'm glad I don't have to misunderstand what Your
universal language is saying to me. Creation all around
whispers and shouts the truth of Your existence. Thank
You for speaking plainly to me. Amen.

BLAMELESS AND INNOCENT IN SPEECH

Who can understand his errors? Cleanse me from secret faults. Keep back Your servant also from presumptuous sins; let them not have dominion over me. Then I shall be blameless, and I shall be innocent of great transgression. Let the words of my mouth and the meditation of my heart be acceptable in Your sight, O LORD, my strength and my Redeemer.

PSALM 19:12–14 NKJV

. . . .

Lord Jesus, when You walked on earth, You used words perfectly. Over and over again, evil men tried to trip You up in Your words or to get You to use the nuances and connotations wrongly. But, of course, they could not fool the Creator of language and the One who sees the intents of our hearts. You always knew just what to say and how to say it. You interacted with so many people with words, and You were sinless in Your speech.

Today I want the prayer of David to be mine: I want my words and the meditation that prompts them to be acceptable and holy in Your sight. In Jesus' name. Amen.

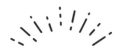

WORDS OF WARNING

[Discretion shall watch over you, understanding shall keep you] to deliver you from the alien woman, from the outsider with her flattering words, who forsakes the husband and guide of her youth and forgets the covenant of her God. For her house sinks down to death and her paths to the spirits [of the dead]. None who go to her return again, neither do they attain or regain the paths of life. So may you walk in the way of good men, and keep to the paths of the [consistently] righteous (the upright, in right standing with God).

PROVERBS 2:16–20 AMPC

O Lord, Your Word contains warnings for us, and they help us keep centered on You. Satan uses other words from other mouths to attract me. The messages that come from him don't tell the truth about the human condition; they whisper that I can sin on the side and get away with it. They tell me, "No one is perfect. You might as well have a little fun while no one is watching."

But I want to walk in the path of goodness—and only by following You can I do that. If I listen to the words of my enemy, I will find myself sinking down to death. But I trust in You—Your words are the plain truth I need. Amen.

PLAIN WORDS OF WISDOM

*Prize Wisdom highly and exalt her, and she will
exalt and promote you; she will bring you to honor
when you embrace her. She shall give to your head
a wreath of gracefulness; a crown of beauty and
glory will she deliver to you. Hear, O my son, and
receive my sayings, and the years of your life shall
be many. I have taught you in the way of skillful and
godly Wisdom [which is comprehensive insight into
the ways and purposes of God]; I have led you in
paths of uprightness. . . . Take firm hold of instruction,
do not let go; guard her, for she is your life.*

<small>PROVERBS 4:8–11, 13 AMPC</small>

Lord God, wisdom is a classic-sounding word. It reminds
me of thick books and libraries, of gray-haired professors
and ivied buildings with towers. These verses speak of
gracefulness, beauty, and glory. They compare wisdom
to a lovely lady.

Our world likes to hear nice words. Affirmation is what
our society prizes. Wisdom is often seen as secondary
to feelings. As a result, many wholesome boundaries are
being sacrificed on the altar of niceness.

Lord, You have never been unkind, but You do speak
truth. And I'm so grateful. Your plain words of wisdom
teach me and hold me fast. Amen.

PLAINSPOKEN

*For my mouth shall utter truth, and wrongdoing
is detestable and loathsome to my lips. All the
words of my mouth are righteous (upright and in
right standing with God); there is nothing contrary
to truth or crooked in them. They are all plain to
him who understands [and opens his heart], and
right to those who find knowledge [and live by it].
Receive my instruction in preference to [striving for]
silver, and knowledge rather than choice gold.*

PROVERBS 8:7–10 AMPC

Lord, I want to be a person of plain speech—the kind of speech that edifies and builds up. I want to use my words to point to Your goodness and help others turn away from evil. Plain, God-honoring speech can bring wealth to those who are careful to use it. The verses above say that Your instruction is better than silver or gold, and no one can take it away.

Father God, the words we speak say so much about us. I want to be known for being plainspoken in the very best way—glorifying You and loving others with my words. Amen.

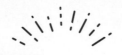

HEEDING REPROOF

He who heeds instruction and correction is [not only himself] in the way of life [but also] is a way of life for others. And he who neglects or refuses reproof [not only himself] goes astray [but also] causes to err and is a path toward ruin for others.... In a multitude of words transgression is not lacking, but he who restrains his lips is prudent.

PROVERBS 10:17, 19 AMPC

Father God, You know the human tendency. You tell us in Your Word how to avoid sin. And sinning with words is probably close to the top of the list of human fallibilities.

Receiving words of instruction and correction from someone else can be difficult. I guess that's pride. I want to be able to do something without being told how, or I may be tempted to react wrongly to reproof. I also struggle not to sin with my words when a conversation goes on and on. Sometimes my curiosity and compassion can turn into cancerous words.

Help me today, Father, to listen to the plain reproof I need but not to fall prey to plain gossip. In Jesus' name. Amen.

A GENTLE TONGUE

*A soft answer turns away wrath, but a harsh word
stirs up anger. The tongue of the wise commends
knowledge, but the mouths of fools pour out folly.
The eyes of the LORD are in every place, keeping
watch on the evil and the good. A gentle tongue
is a tree of life, but perverseness in it breaks the
spirit. A fool despises his father's instruction, but
whoever heeds reproof is prudent. In the house of
the righteous there is much treasure, but trouble
befalls the income of the wicked. The lips of the
wise spread knowledge; not so the hearts of fools.*

PROVERBS 15:1–7 ESV

Dear Lord, as I face my day, I turn to Your Word for
instruction on how to use my words well. Sometimes
I want to bulldoze through without taking the time to
choose my words. But I know that You want me to be
focused on honoring You with my words, and part of
that is thinking about how they affect others. Words can
be painful and destructive, or they can be refreshing
and life-giving. Sometimes strong words are needed,
but the words don't have to be harsh. Please remind me
of this truth over and over again, Lord. Amen.

WORDS TO PROD ME ALONG

The words of the wise are like goads, and like nails firmly fixed are the collected sayings; they are given by one Shepherd. My son, beware of anything beyond these.... The end of the matter; all has been heard. Fear God and keep his commandments, for this is the whole duty of man. For God will bring every deed into judgment, with every secret thing, whether good or evil.

ECCLESIASTES 12:11–14 ESV

Heavenly Father, thank You for being my Shepherd. You know what I need. Sometimes You let me rest beside peaceful streams. But other times You nudge me to get up and keep moving. And You often use the words of others to do that. Thank You for the friends and mentors in my life who know me well and who stay in touch with me when I need it most. Their words are like the point of a cattle prod to my spirit, urging me forward and out of my areas of comfort.

Today, Lord, let me be an encourager to someone else. I know that someday You will bring all my deeds to judgment, and I want the words I say to be ones that remind others to revere You and keep Your commandments. Amen.

WORDS THAT PROFIT

And he said to all, "If anyone would come after me, let him deny himself and take up his cross daily and follow me. For whoever would save his life will lose it, but whoever loses his life for my sake will save it. For what does it profit a man if he gains the whole world and loses or forfeits himself? For whoever is ashamed of me and of my words, of him will the Son of Man be ashamed when he comes in his glory and the glory of the Father and of the holy angels.

LUKE 9:23–26 ESV

Lord Jesus, I'm thankful for what You did for me on the cross. But help me remember that real gratitude takes the form of action. It isn't enough for me to feel grateful for Your sacrifice; I need to let my gratitude turn into behavior that proves my love for You. I don't want You to be ashamed of me someday before the Father in heaven, and so I want to live unreservedly and unashamedly for You right now. Amen.

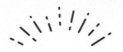

A PATTERN OF SOUND WORDS

But I am not ashamed, for I know whom I have believed, and I am convinced that he is able to guard until that day what has been entrusted to me. Follow the pattern of the sound words that you have heard from me, in the faith and love that are in Christ Jesus. By the Holy Spirit who dwells within us, guard the good deposit entrusted to you.

2 TIMOTHY 1:12–14 ESV

Dear Lord, humans are predictable in many ways. We like patterns of behavior; our brains are wired to get into a comfortable routine and stay there. But sometimes we get stuck in bad patterns—patterns that are detrimental instead of beneficial. Before I came to You for salvation, I had some bad patterns in my life. But I am so thankful that You can release us from the chains of destructive thoughts and destructive ways of doing things.

Another way my life has changed is that I now do my best to follow the sound words that make up a healthy pattern of service to others. I know that the way to guard my spiritual life is to follow the words You left us. Please help me do that, Lord! Amen.

THE POWER OF WORDS

But you must remember, beloved, the predictions of the apostles of our Lord Jesus Christ. They said to you, "In the last time there will be scoffers, following their own ungodly passions." It is these who cause divisions, worldly people, devoid of the Spirit. But you, beloved, building yourselves up in your most holy faith and praying in the Holy Spirit, keep yourselves in the love of God, waiting for the mercy of our Lord Jesus Christ that leads to eternal life.

JUDE 1:17–21 ESV

. . . .

Father God, words are the material that comprise much of our joy and much of our sadness. Words communicate our emotions and help us get to know each other. Prophets and pastors use words to warn us of things to come—things for which to prepare. Others use words like dividing walls, putting up barriers between people. You have called me to build up myself and others in the faith, praying and keeping myself close to Your love and eternal life. When I look at my daily words through this lens, I can see the great power of words. Use me today, as I use my words for You. Amen.

TRUSTWORTHY AND TRUE WORDS

And he who was seated on the throne said, "Behold, I am making all things new." Also he said, "Write this down, for these words are trustworthy and true." And he said to me, "It is done! I am the Alpha and the Omega, the beginning and the end. To the thirsty I will give from the spring of the water of life without payment. The one who conquers will have this heritage, and I will be his God and he will be my son."

REVELATION 21:5–7 ESV

• •

Dear Lord in heaven, someday, by Your grace, I will see You seated on a throne, and You will make all things new. I will rejoice at the new meanings of words and the new joy to share. Lord, You were the beginning of our earthly story when You created the world, and You will be the ending of it when You create a new heaven and earth. Because You have conquered death, we can share in the heritage of unending life and be adopted into Your family forever. Thank You for writing down these incredible, joy-giving words that help me look forward to my future with You. Amen

A Mind Set on Peace

THE BLESSING OF THE LORD

The voice of the LORD is over the waters; the God of glory thunders, the LORD, over many waters. The voice of the LORD is powerful; the voice of the LORD is full of majesty.... The voice of the LORD makes the deer give birth and strips the forests bare, and in his temple all cry, "Glory!" The LORD sits enthroned over the flood; the LORD sits enthroned as king forever. May the LORD give strength to his people! May the LORD bless his people with peace!

PSALM 29:3–4, 9–11 ESV

Heavenly Father, everything around me today seems chaotic. But I remember that *You* are peace. You control the waters, the winds, the wild animals, and all of nature. Mankind gets so stressed worrying about how to save the oceans and the trees and the endangered species. And all the time, You have them firmly in hand. And you tell us not to concern ourselves with Your job—managing the universe. You tell us to concentrate on our job—obeying Your voice just like everything else You created. Thank You, Lord, that I can rest in Your peace. Amen.

DELIVERANCE AND PEACE

Depart from evil and do good; seek, inquire for,
and crave peace and pursue (go after) it! The eyes
of the Lord are toward the [uncompromisingly]
righteous and His ears are open to their cry....
When the righteous cry for help, the Lord hears, and
delivers them out of all their distress and troubles....
Many evils confront the [consistently] righteous,
but the Lord delivers him out of them all.

PSALM 34:14–15, 17, 19 AMPC

. . . .

Lord God, today I'm reading that You want me to crave and pursue peace. I know that true peace originates with You. All the other types of peace are fake and short lived. Only knowing You and following Your way of doing things really bring peace.

Thank You for the examples of Your servants in the Bible; I can read about their lives and see how they found peace. Lord, Noah found peace in the great flood because he obeyed Your command and built an ark that became his means of rescue. Daniel found peace in a den of lions because he trusted in You in every circumstance. If You can keep Your servants safe in those types of conditions, I know You can give me peace in mine. Amen.

MEEKNESS BRINGS PEACE

Be still and rest in the Lord; wait for Him and patiently lean yourself upon Him; fret not yourself because of him who prospers in his way, because of the man who brings wicked devices to pass.... For yet a little while, and the evildoers will be no more; though you look with care where they used to be, they will not be found. But the meek [in the end] shall inherit the earth and shall delight themselves in the abundance of peace.

PSALM 37:7, 10–11 AMPC

. . . .

Dear Lord, sometimes I have the wrong idea about the word *meekness*. It sounds like weakness. But when I read that Moses, the deliverer of the Old Testament, was called the meekest man on earth, and then I read about the meekness of Jesus, the Great Deliverer, I know that being meek is not for the weak but for the strong.

The evildoers who seem so mighty will one day be no more; they only have strength in themselves, and that's not the kind that will last for eternity. But those who are meek in Your name have true power, and someday they will also have abundant peace. Amen.

A HAPPY ENDING

*Mark the blameless man and behold the upright,
for there is a happy end for the man of peace. As for
transgressors, they shall be destroyed together; in
the end the wicked shall be cut off. But the salvation
of the [consistently] righteous is of the Lord; He
is their Refuge and secure Stronghold in the time
of trouble. And the Lord helps them and delivers
them; He delivers them from the wicked and saves
them, because they trust and take refuge in Him.*

PSALM 37:37–40 AMPC

Dear God, I love happy endings. They remind me that You are in control of the universe and that someday You will bring about the best ending to the earthly story. You dwell in eternity, and those who put their trust in You will live there too.

The plot of this old world seems to get more chaotic all the time, but I know that You have the pen firmly in Your hand. You are writing the masterpiece.

The ending of my personal chapter may come before I think I'm ready; but if You are in control, it will be all right. Thank You for being my refuge and my stronghold. Amen.

REDEEMED AND RELIEVED

As for me, I will call upon God, and the Lord will save me. Evening and morning and at noon will I utter my complaint and moan and sigh, and He will hear my voice. He has redeemed my life in peace from the battle that was against me [so that none came near me], for they were many who strove with me. . . . Cast your burden on the Lord [releasing the weight of it] and He will sustain you; He will never allow the [consistently] righteous to be moved (made to slip, fall, or fail).

PSALM 55:16–18, 22 AMPC

. . . .

O God, You hear me when I call out to You. You have redeemed my life. I know I don't have to slip or fall when I'm holding Your hand.

Thank You for the testimonies of those who have gone before me. I have heard them testify to Your unfailing care. I know that, like them, I can cast my burden on You and You will help me carry it. Right now, I release onto You the weight that is bogging me down. I can't have peace until I know that You have charge of it. Thank You for being my God. Amen.

PEACE WHEN THE MOON IS GONE

In His [Christ's] days shall the [uncompromisingly] righteous flourish and peace abound till there is a moon no longer. He [Christ] shall have dominion also from sea to sea and from the River [Euphrates] to the ends of the earth. . . . For He delivers the needy when he calls out, the poor also and him who has no helper. He will have pity on the poor and weak and needy and will save the lives of the needy. He will redeem their lives from oppression and fraud and violence, and precious and costly shall their blood be in His sight.

PSALM 72:7–8, 12–14 AMPC

. . . .

Lord, I don't know Your timetable for all that will happen to the earth. But I know that one day You will create a new heaven and earth and rearrange the order, putting things back to Your original intent for us and our world. You will reign from sea to sea, and nothing will be out of place.

O God, right now You are at work, reaching down to the needy and having compassion on the lost. You want to redeem them so that someday they may share in Your peace. Thank You for being a merciful God. Amen.

PEACE IN YOUR LAW

Great peace have they who love Your law; nothing
shall offend them or make them stumble. I am hoping
and waiting [eagerly] for Your salvation, O Lord, and
I do Your commandments. Your testimonies have I
kept [hearing, receiving, loving, and obeying them]; I
love them exceedingly! I have observed Your precepts
and Your testimonies, for all my ways are [fully known]
before You. . . . Let Your hand be ready to help me, for
I have chosen Your precepts. I have longed for Your
salvation, O Lord, and Your law is my delight. Let me
live that I may praise You, and let Your decrees help me.

Psalm 119:165–168, 173–175 AMPC

. . . .

Dear God, often we mistakenly think that peace comes from unrestrained freedom, from the absence of laws. But really, the greatest peace comes when I am in harmony with Your laws. As I learn Your commands and do them, I am filled with satisfaction and joy. When my ways (my attitudes and actions and thoughts) are all known to You—laid out before You on the conveyor belt of life—I find that I am most content. I long for Your salvation. In Jesus' name. Amen.

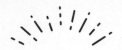

JERUSALEM, THE EPICENTER OF FUTURE PEACE

Pray for the peace of Jerusalem! "May they be secure who love you! Peace be within your walls and security within your towers!" For my brothers and companions' sake I will say, "Peace be within you!" For the sake of the house of the LORD our God, I will seek your good.

PSALM 122:6–9 ESV

Lord Jesus, You grieved for the city of Jerusalem, the Holy City. You grieved for its people. You grieved for its destruction. You, the Son of God who came to bring peace, knew that Jerusalem would never have it until they accepted You.

You have told us to pray that peace might reign in Jerusalem. Because the Jews were the human genealogy through which You brought Jesus, they are dear to You and Your covenant with them is still in effect. Someday their eyes will be opened, and they will understand that You are the One for whom they have been waiting. Have mercy on Jerusalem, Lord. Amen.

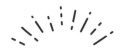

BLESSING AND PEACE

Blessed is everyone who fears the LORD, who walks in his ways! You shall eat the fruit of the labor of your hands; you shall be blessed, and it shall be well with you.... The LORD bless you from Zion! May you see the prosperity of Jerusalem all the days of your life! May you see your children's children! Peace be upon Israel!

PSALM 128:1–2, 5–6 ESV

. . . .

O Lord, often You use earthly labors to bring us good things in life. You bless the work we do with our hands and provide for our needs through it. The delicious fruit of honest work is a blessing. And when Jerusalem is restored to its glory one day, the people will experience prosperity and peace.

These verses mention grandchildren, and You know, Lord, how I want to be a godly influence in those little lives You've given to my children. Show me how to teach them these important truths. I thank You for Your radical and abundant peace. In Jesus' name. Amen.

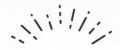

REMEMBER THE TEACHING!

*My son, do not forget my teaching, but let your
heart keep my commandments, for length of days
and years of life and peace they will add to you.
Let not steadfast love and faithfulness forsake
you; bind them around your neck; write them on
the tablet of your heart. So you will find favor and
good success in the sight of God and man.*

PROVERBS 3:1–4 ESV

Dear Father, the way to have a successful and peaceful
life is to keep Your words close to my heart. That's why
it's so important for me to spend time in Your Word and
then to gather with other believers and hear it taught.
There are so many other messages in our culture, and my
mind gets foggy with all the information. But Your truth is
something I want to stay clear in my thoughts.

I ask You to put people in my path today who will help
me stay focused on You. Thank You for orchestrating
even the tiniest details of my life, reminding me of Your
steadfast love and faithfulness. Help me to remember the
teaching of Your Word and to keep Your commandments.
I ask this in Jesus' name. Amen.

ENEMIES AT PEACE

Commit your work to the LORD, and your plans will be established. The LORD has made everything for its purpose, even the wicked for the day of trouble. Everyone who is arrogant in heart is an abomination to the LORD; be assured, he will not go unpunished. By steadfast love and faithfulness iniquity is atoned for, and by the fear of the LORD one turns away from evil. When a man's ways please the LORD, he makes even his enemies to be at peace with him.

PROVERBS 16:3–7 ESV

. . . .

Lord, I hope I don't have any enemies. I don't like the idea of someone not wanting to be around me—or worse, hoping that something terrible happens to me! Hatred and enemies go hand in hand. I know You have changed my heart; because of Your grace, I don't harbor hatred for anyone. You have turned me away from evil and toward good—toward You. Please help me today to keep my heart turned to what it right. I want to commit all I do to You. Then I can trust that the peace You've promised will surround me. Amen.

NO END TO HIS PEACE

The people who walked in darkness have seen a great light; those who dwelt in a land of deep darkness, on them has light shone.... For to us a child is born, to us a son is given; and the government shall be upon his shoulder, and his name shall be called Wonderful Counselor, Mighty God, Everlasting Father, Prince of Peace. Of the increase of his government and of peace there will be no end, on the throne of David and over his kingdom, to establish it and to uphold it with justice and with righteousness from this time forth and forevermore. The zeal of the LORD of hosts will do this.

ISAIAH 9:2, 6–7 ESV

. . . .

Lord Jesus, You are the very Prince of Peace. These majestic words are usually quoted or sung at Christmastime. But I'm glad they are true all year through. The government of the whole world rests on Your shoulders. The scepter of power is in Your hand. Your death has brought about an unsurpassed, unending peace. You will uphold Your kingdom with justice and righteousness forever. I am so grateful You've chosen me to be Your child. Amen.

EVERLASTING ROCK OF PEACE

In that day this song will be sung in the land of Judah: "We have a strong city; he sets up salvation as walls and bulwarks. Open the gates, that the righteous nation that keeps faith may enter in. You keep him in perfect peace whose mind is stayed on you, because he trusts in you. Trust in the LORD forever, for the LORD GOD is an everlasting rock.

ISAIAH 26:1–4 ESV

Heavenly Father, I'm glad You are my everlasting bulwark against the floods of this world. You set up the strong city; You keep the gates. And You will open them to the righteous and keep me in perfect peace if I redirect my anxious thoughts to You. Help me to trust in You, Lord, as I go throughout my day and evening. Watch over me and convict me when I start to worry. I pray in Jesus' name. Amen.

RIGHTEOUSNESS BRINGS PEACE

Then justice will dwell in the wilderness, and righteousness remain in the fruitful field. The work of righteousness will be peace, and the effect of righteousness, quietness and assurance forever. My people will dwell in a peaceful habitation, in secure dwellings, and in quiet resting places, though hail comes down on the forest, and the city is brought low in humiliation. Blessed are you who sow beside all waters, who send out freely the feet of the ox and the donkey.

ISAIAH 32:16–20 NKJV

. . . .

Father God, I have seen the damage caused by high winds and hail sweeping through a forest. Your Word contrasts this chaos with the peaceful habitation of those who have put their trust in You. Those who sow generously and who treat their animals well are often the ones who, whether they live in the wilderness or near fertile fields, have found a way to stay focused on Your goodness. Thank You for allowing me to know individuals who model the truth that righteousness brings peace. I, too, want to be a good reflection of You. Amen.

WELL-BEING AND CALAMITY

"For the sake of my servant Jacob, and Israel my chosen, I call you by your name, I name you, though you do not know me. I am the LORD, and there is no other, besides me there is no God; I equip you, though you do not know me, that people may know, from the rising of the sun and from the west, that there is none besides me; I am the LORD, and there is no other. I form light and create darkness; I make well-being and create calamity; I am the LORD, who does all these things."

ISAIAH 45:4–7 ESV

. . . .

Heavenly Father, You have called me by my name! You know all there is to know about me. And I continue to learn more about You. You created both light and darkness; You bring order to our world; yet You are the One who confused the languages at Babel. You want to give us peace in our lives. It is only our own selfishness or sense of self-importance that brings to mind thoughts of wanting to go our own way. I reject those thoughts and choose to reestablish a mindset of following Christ. Thank You for never giving up on me. Amen.

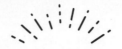

WATCHMEN AND WASTE PLACES

How beautiful upon the mountains are the feet of him who brings good news, who publishes peace, who brings good news of happiness, who publishes salvation, who says to Zion, "Your God reigns." The voice of your watchmen—they lift up their voice; together they sing for joy; for eye to eye they see the return of the LORD to Zion. Break forth together into singing, you waste places of Jerusalem, for the LORD has comforted his people; he has redeemed Jerusalem.

ISAIAH 52:7–9 ESV

Dear God, You want me to be a publisher of peace. You want to take my thoughts and ways of speaking and put me to work proclaiming the Good News to those who haven't heard. You can redeem and restore what is broken. And You have more than enough peace to go around. Today, God, as I interact with my family and coworkers and even strangers, make me an instrument of real peace. In Jesus' name I pray. Amen.

HIS PUNISHMENT BROUGHT OUR PEACE

Surely he has borne our griefs and carried our sorrows; yet we esteemed him stricken, smitten by God, and afflicted. But he was pierced for our transgressions; he was crushed for our iniquities; upon him was the chastisement that brought us peace, and with his wounds we are healed.

ISAIAH 53:4–5 ESV

• •

Lord Jesus, thank You for bearing the cross all the way to Golgotha. Thank You for not throwing it off when the suffering became unbearable. Thank You for being willing to be pierced and crushed. The blows that You suffered and the wounds that You endured became the channel that brought peace to me.

Lord, I remember the man named Simon whom the soldiers commissioned to carry Your cross when You collapsed under the weight. He knew only the physical weight of the wood; but You knew the intense spiritual weight as You carried the sins of us all on Your shoulders.

Thank You for bringing peace to me through Your sacrificial act of redemption. Amen.

AN EXTRAORDINARY ENSEMBLE

"For you shall go out in joy and be led forth in peace; the mountains and the hills before you shall break forth into singing, and all the trees of the field shall clap their hands. Instead of the thorn shall come up the cypress; instead of the brier shall come up the myrtle; and it shall make a name for the LORD, an everlasting sign that shall not be cut off."

ISAIAH 55:12–13 ESV

Today, Lord, I'm grateful for the beautiful imagery in Your Word that helps me put a tangible meaning to spiritual truths. As I think about the mountains and the hills beginning to sing and the trees clapping their hands, I realize You are telling me that the whole of nature responds to Your voice and Your works. They celebrate when You move in power. And so should we! The only thing really worth cheering for is Your greatness, revealed through Your love and holiness and through everything You have made. The singing hills and clapping trees form an extraordinary ensemble in their praise of You. May I join in as all creation lifts a chorus of praise to You! Amen.

PEACE IN THE ABSENCE OF EVIL

*Then they went into Capernaum, and immediately
on the Sabbath He entered the synagogue and
taught. And they were astonished at His teaching,
for He taught them as one having authority, and
not as the scribes. Now there was a man in their
synagogue with an unclean spirit. And he cried out,
saying, "Let us alone! What have we to do with You,
Jesus of Nazareth? Did You come to destroy us? I
know who You are—the Holy One of God!" But Jesus
rebuked him, saying, "Be quiet, and come out of him!"
And when the unclean spirit had convulsed him and
cried out with a loud voice, he came out of him.*

MARK 1:21–26 NKJV

Lord Jesus, You are the Peace Giver. This story about a
man held captive by evil reminds me of the evil going on
in the world today. While we don't see the overt signs of
oppression like You did when You walked the earth, we
do see the effect of this spiritual warfare in the addictions
that grip our loved ones. Lord, even the demonic spirits
have to acknowledge that You are Lord. Thank You that
Your power is able to wipe out evil and set people free.
And when the evil is gone, You replace it with a fresh and
filling peace. Amen.

THE SEA SPEAKER

And a great windstorm arose, and the waves beat into the boat, so that it was already filling. But He was in the stern, asleep on a pillow. And they awoke Him and said to Him, "Teacher, do You not care that we are perishing?" Then He arose and rebuked the wind, and said to the sea, "Peace, be still!" And the wind ceased and there was a great calm. But He said to them, "Why are you so fearful? How is it that you have no faith?" And they feared exceedingly, and said to one another, "Who can this be, that even the wind and the sea obey Him!"

MARK 4:37–41 NKJV

Dear Jesus, I wonder what it was like to be in that little boat on the Sea of Galilee! A storm arose quickly, and the disciples were afraid. You were asleep. The creation You made could not harm You, and so the disciples were safe even though they didn't know it! Sometimes I'm very much like them—afraid of what might happen to me when, all along, Your presence keeps me safe. Thank You for speaking peace even to rogue waves. Amen.

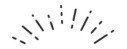

DAYSPRING OF PEACE

"And you, child, will be called the prophet of the Highest; for you will go before the face of the Lord to prepare His ways, to give knowledge of salvation to His people by the remission of their sins, through the tender mercy of our God, with which the Dayspring from on high has visited us; to give light to those who sit in darkness and the shadow of death, to guide our feet into the way of peace."

LUKE 1:76–79 NKJV

Lord Jesus, what a wonder that You became a tiny baby in order to enter our earth! Supernaturally, You laid aside Your awe-inspiring greatness and became flesh like us so that one day we could be glorified like You. We will never be divine, but we can partake of Your glory and grace because You were willing to grow to manhood and die on the cross. The prophecy of Zechariah calls You the Dayspring, who gives light and guides us into peace. Thank You, Jesus. Amen.

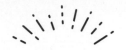

BACK HOME IN PEACE

But Jesus said, "Somebody touched Me, for I perceived power going out from Me." Now when the woman saw that she was not hidden, she came trembling; and falling down before Him, she declared to Him in the presence of all the people the reason she had touched Him and how she was healed immediately. And He said to her, "Daughter, be of good cheer; your faith has made you well. Go in peace."

LUKE 8:46–48 NKJV

Dear Lord Jesus, You were approachable when You walked the earth. And yet this woman was afraid to acknowledge that she had touched Your garment. Maybe she didn't want to be laughed at by those who knew she'd already tried every new miracle remedy anyone recommended. Maybe she was afraid You would be angry. Maybe she just wanted to rejoice quietly. But You comforted her and sent her home in peace. You are the Healer and Peace Giver. Amen.

THE DIVINE LEFTOVER—PEACE

"These things I have spoken to you while being present with you. But the Helper, the Holy Spirit, whom the Father will send in My name, He will teach you all things, and bring to your remembrance all things that I said to you. Peace I leave with you, My peace I give to you; not as the world gives do I give to you. Let not your heart be troubled, neither let it be afraid."

JOHN 14:25–27 NKJV

Dear Lord, when I was a child, I didn't like leftovers, but the kind of leftover You give is different. You left Your disciples with the essence of Your message—peace. You wanted them to know that You have accomplished peace between God and man through the cross. And You wanted them to experience this assurance in their hearts. Thank You for giving it to me too. When my heart begins to fear, I can again read these words—preserved for me—and rejoice. Amen.

PEACE FROM THE SHEPHERD

*Therefore, having been justified by faith,
we have peace with God through our Lord
Jesus Christ, through whom also we have
access by faith into this grace in which we
stand, and rejoice in hope of the glory of God.
And not only that, but we also glory in tribulations,
knowing that tribulation produces perseverance;
and perseverance, character; and character, hope.*

ROMANS 5:1–4 NKJV

Dear Father in heaven, nothing can take the place of Your peace in my heart. I was a sinner, far from You, but You found me and gave me hope. The Bible compares You to a good shepherd looking for a lost sheep. You found me tangled in sin and despair, and You reached down through the briars of doubt and disbelief and pulled me off the cliff where I trembled in fear. You brushed me off, held me close, and started the journey home. Once I felt the love in Your hands and heart, I could do nothing but surrender. Thank You, Jesus, for rescuing me. Amen.

NOT VENGEANCE BUT PEACE

Repay no one evil for evil. Have regard for good
things in the sight of all men. If it is possible, as
much as depends on you, live peaceably with all
men. Beloved, do not avenge yourselves, but rather
give place to wrath; for it is written, "Vengeance
is Mine, I will repay," says the Lord. . . . Do not be
overcome by evil, but overcome evil with good.

ROMANS 12:17–19, 21 NKJV

. . . .

Dear Lord, the true test of a servant is whether she follows her Master's commands. In Your Word, You left us the command of love. You told us not to get even but to love harder. You illustrated how to go the extra mile and overlook injustices. You modeled mercy for us as You forgave Your tormentors while You hung on the cross. Your will for us is that we should not be angry avengers but rather calm forgivers. And we need Your grace to be able to accomplish this. Thank You that Your supply of enabling grace will never be on back order. Amen.

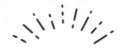

PEACE AND CRUSHING

And the God of peace will crush Satan under your feet shortly. The grace of our Lord Jesus Christ be with you. Amen. . . . Now to Him who is able to establish you according to my gospel and the preaching of Jesus Christ, according to the revelation of the mystery kept secret since the world began but now made manifest, and by the prophetic Scriptures made known to all nations, according to the commandment of the everlasting God, for obedience to the faith—to God, alone wise, be glory through Jesus Christ forever. Amen.

ROMANS 16:20, 25–27 NKJV

Creator God, when time began for our planet in the Garden, You placed a mysterious tree in the center for the testing of love. Ultimately, Adam and Eve failed that test when they chose their wants over Your will. And then they hid from You and tried to get off the hook by blaming the serpent. But You, God, already knew what had happened. You promised the trembling couple that the serpent would be crushed someday. And he was. He lies at Your feet, defeated. Thank You for sending the Prince of Peace to strike the death blow to evil. Amen.

THE RECONCILER

*But now in Christ Jesus you who once were far off
have been brought near by the blood of Christ. For
He Himself is our peace, who has made both one,
and has broken down the middle wall of separation,
having abolished in His flesh the enmity, that is, the
law of commandments contained in ordinances, so as
to create in Himself one new man from the two, thus
making peace, and that He might reconcile them both
to God in one body through the cross, thereby putting
to death the enmity. And He came and preached peace
to you who were afar off and to those who were near.*

Ephesians 2:13–17 NKJV

Lord Jesus, You didn't just bring peace to earth: You
are peace. You brought together God and sinful man
because You hung in the middle on the cross and broke
down the wall of separation. Your perfect sacrifice made
reconciliation possible. And through Your sacrifice, both
those who were near, the Jews, and those who were far
off, the non-Jews, have been called to experience Your
profoundly liberating redemption. I praise You for what
You did on Calvary. Amen.

UNITY AND PEACE

I, therefore, the prisoner of the Lord, beseech you to walk worthy of the calling with which you were called, with all lowliness and gentleness, with longsuffering, bearing with one another in love, endeavoring to keep the unity of the Spirit in the bond of peace. There is one body and one Spirit, just as you were called in one hope of your calling; one Lord, one faith, one baptism; one God and Father of all, who is above all, and through all, and in you all.

EPHESIANS 4:1–6 NKJV

Lord God, a lot of confusion surrounds the idea of unity, it seems. Some people think it means identical perspectives and preferences and interpretations. But it doesn't. It means that we have unified around one Lord and faith and baptism. We will probably never see everything through the same lens, and that's okay. But we can be at peace with one another, because You enable us to love each other through Your Spirit who lives within us.

Help me today, Lord, to allow the Holy Spirit, who dwells in me, to remind me to bear with others in love and do everything I can to keep the peace. In Jesus' name. Amen.

THE BODYGUARD

Rejoice in the Lord always. Again I will say, rejoice!
Let your gentleness be known to all men. The Lord is
at hand. Be anxious for nothing, but in everything by
prayer and supplication, with thanksgiving, let your
requests be made known to God; and the peace of
God, which surpasses all understanding, will guard
your hearts and minds through Christ Jesus.

PHILIPPIANS 4:4–7 NKJV

Dear Father, this passage is often quoted in the Christian community. But quoting it and living it can be separate issues. It is so hard not to worry. But I want to honor Your Word in my everyday life. You tell me not to worry but to commit everything to You in prayer. And You promise that Your peace will stand watch (be a bodyguard) over my heart and mind. Lord, the bodyguards I've seen take their job very seriously. They are there to stand between the threat and the person being guarded. I think that's the picture of this peace. It stands between, heading off the worry before it shows up. I thank You, Lord, for teaching me more about trusting. Amen.

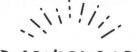

HARMONIOUS PEACE

Let the peace of Christ rule in your hearts, remembering that as members of the same body you are called to live in harmony, and never forget to be thankful for what God has done for you. Let Christ's teaching live in your hearts, making you rich in the true wisdom. Teach and help one another along the right road with your psalms and hymns and Christian songs, singing God's praises with joyful hearts. And whatever you may have to do, do everything in the name of the Lord Jesus, thanking God the Father through him.

COLOSSIANS 3:15–17 PHILLIPS

O Lord, thank You for the Body of Christ, the Church. You didn't design us to live in isolation, and so the family of God—with You as our Elder Brother—is the place where we experience optimum growth and inspiration. Sometimes that growth means that our boundaries have to be moved a bit and our notions have to be challenged. But You want us to approach it all from a desire to live in harmony. And You tell us to sing to one another and together. It's hard to make music with someone you aren't speaking to! Thank You for giving us this practical means of living out our Christian love. Amen.

HOLY AND KEPT IN INTEGRITY

Never damp the fire of the Spirit, and never despise what is spoken in the name of the Lord. By all means use your judgement, and hold on to whatever is really good. Steer clear of evil in any form. May the God of peace make you holy through and through. May you be kept in soul and mind and body in spotless integrity until the coming of our Lord Jesus Christ. He who calls you is utterly faithful and he will finish what he has set out to do.

1 Thessalonians 5:19–24 Phillips

Father in heaven, I need Your holiness to be mine today. This passage tells me that You, the God of peace, can make me holy through and through. You are the Faithful One who can do it. I know I won't have inner peace until the clamor of selfish reason is replaced by the melody of righteousness in You. I want to avoid evil in any form and cling to what is good. Thank You for Your Holy Spirit who instructs me and warns me of danger; help me never to dampen His light by my resistance. I ask all of this in Jesus' name. Amen.

PEACE INSTEAD OF BITTERNESS

*Let it be your ambition to live at peace with all
men and to achieve holiness "without which no
man shall see the Lord". Be careful that none of
you fails to respond to the grace which God gives,
for if he does there can very easily spring up in
him a bitter spirit which is not only bad in itself
but can also poison the lives of many others.*

HEBREWS 12:14–15 PHILLIPS

Father God, I don't want to be a bitter person. I've been around some people like that. Their bitterness is an infection that spreads to every part of their lives. They have a spirit of cancer about them, like a malignancy taking over their hearts and souls and emotions.

But You, Lord, call us to respond to Your grace, which enables us to live in peace with others, even when they have wounded us. You forgave Your crucifiers, and You can help me forgive those who try to destroy me.

I want to have a holy heart so that I can see You someday. I know bitterness is not a holy trait. Today I surrender myself to You. In Jesus' name. Amen.

THE SHEPHERD OF PEACE

Now the God of peace, who brought back from the dead that great shepherd of the sheep, our Lord Jesus, by the blood of the everlasting agreement, equip you thoroughly for the doing of his will! May he effect in you everything that pleases him through Jesus Christ, to whom be glory for ever and ever.

HEBREWS 13:20–21 PHILLIPS

Dear Jesus, when I was little, I was intrigued by the Sunday school pictures of Jesus as the Good Shepherd leaning out to rescue a lamb. The look on His face was one of concern and love and yet complete confidence that He could change things if the sheep cooperated. I know a picture could never really capture the love in Your heart, and so today I thank You for going after lost things. You won't give up until You have exhausted all effort to keep the wayward lamb in Your fold. The only way for that lamb not to be cared for is by an act of outright rebellion—following a stubborn will right out of the fold.

Lord, I'm glad I don't have to wander but can stay safe and secure with the Shepherd. His everlasting covenant is effective. I'm so grateful. Amen.

WISE PEACEMAKERS

The wisdom that comes from God is first utterly pure, then peace-loving, gentle, approachable, full of tolerant thoughts and kindly actions, with no breath of favouritism or hint of hypocrisy. And the wise are peace-makers who go on quietly sowing for a harvest of righteousness—in other people and in themselves.

JAMES 3:17–18 PHILLIPS

Dear Father God, nothing compares to the feeling of being at peace with God and man. Thank You for making such peace possible through the life and death of Jesus. You want to reap a great harvest of righteousness; every person alive is called to join the celebration of eternal life.

Lord, I remember the parable of the two sons—one prodigal and one pompous. Both were in need of heavenly wisdom so that they might interact with others out of peace. As I go out into my day, I don't know whom I will meet or what they will need. But You do. Give me, Father, the grace to be a peacemaker and a worker for the harvest of righteousness. In Jesus' name. Amen.

FAMILY TIES

To sum up, you should all be of one mind living like brothers with true love and sympathy for each other, generous and courteous at all times. Never pay back a bad turn with a bad turn or an insult with another insult, but on the contrary pay back with good. For this is your calling—to do good and one day to inherit all the goodness of God. For: "He who would love life and see good days, let him refrain his tongue from evil, and his lips from speaking guile: let him turn away from evil and do good; let him seek peace and pursue it. For the eyes of the Lord are on the righteous, and his ears are open to their prayers; but the face of the Lord is against those who do evil."

1 Peter 3:8–12 Phillips

. . . .

O Lord, when I was growing up, I squabbled with my siblings. But as I grew older, I realized how blessed I was to have them in my life. Sure, at times they still irritated me, but I began to see that they would be there for me through all the ups and downs. That's the way You want me to see my fellow believers. They are my family, and we are meant to do life together. Amen.

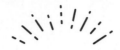

CLEAN AND BLAMELESS
AND AT PEACE

What sort of people ought you to be? Surely men of good and holy character, who live expecting and earnestly longing for the coming of the day of God. True, this day will mean that the heavens will disappear in fire and the elements disintegrate in fearful heat, but our hopes are set not on these but on the new Heaven and the new earth which he has promised us, and in which nothing but good shall live. Because, my dear friends, you have a hope like this before you, I urge you to make certain that such a day would find you at peace with God and man, clean and blameless in his sight.

2 Peter 3:11–14 Phillips

Father, there are many scoffers today who question whether You will return. They cast doubts on Your creative work in the beginning too. But You call us to live with expectation and longing. The things You have said will come true, just as the flood really did arrive in Noah's day. And this time, You will use fire instead of water. The earth will be cleansed of all the pollution of sin. And You will make a new place for us to live for eternity. I look forward to that, Lord. Amen.

A Mind Set on Parenting

NO RESPECT FOR PARENTS

They scoffed at duty to parents, they mocked at learning, recognised no obligations of honour, lost all natural affection, and had no use for mercy. More than this—being well aware of God's pronouncement that all who do these things deserve to die, they not only continued their own practices, but did not hesitate to give their thorough approval to others who did the same.

ROMANS 1:30-32 PHILLIPS

Dear Lord, I've heard the popular notion that respect must be earned before it can be given. I think it's wonderful when someone deserves respect; but Lord, Your Word commands me to respect my parents no matter their personal traits. Showing respect doesn't mean I should willingly allow myself to be harmed if they are truly bad parents. But it does mean I can respect them as persons created by You, and I can honor the position they hold as my father and mother.

If respect were granted only to those who earned it, few of us would make the grade. Of course, we should do everything in our power to be worthy of honor, but please remind us that there is a place in our homes and churches and society for respect to be given to whom it is due. Amen.

A CHILD'S DUTY

Let Christ's teaching live in your hearts, making you rich in the true wisdom. Teach and help one another along the right road with your psalms and hymns and Christian songs, singing God's praises with joyful hearts. And whatever you may have to do, do everything in the name of the Lord Jesus, thanking God the Father through him.... As for you children, your duty is to obey your parents, for at your age this is one of the best things you can do to show your love for God.

Colossians 3:16–17, 20 Phillips

Dear heavenly Father, we don't hear much about obedience these days. We hear a lot about giving children choices, using persuasion, and implementing "ignoring" techniques. But the Bible tells children outright to obey their parents. And yes, the context refers to loving parents, not abusive ones. But we have to accept the statement in the vein in which it was given.

Children must be taught by their parents that obedience is the first step in self-control. Parents must require obedience, not as a choice, but as a matter of fact. Thank You, Father, for teaching me that obedience to the voice of Your Holy Spirit is my duty as well. Amen.

EARLY LEARNING

It was by faith that Moses was hidden by his parents for three months after his birth, for they saw that he was an exceptional child and refused to be daunted by the king's decree that all male children should be drowned. It was also by faith that Moses himself when grown up refused to be called the son of Pharaoh's daughter. He preferred sharing the burden of God's people to enjoying the temporary advantages of alliance with a sinful nation. He considered the "reproach of Christ" more precious than all the wealth of Egypt, for he looked steadily at the ultimate, not the immediate, reward.

HEBREWS 11:23–26 PHILLIPS

· ·

Dear Lord, few parenting stories have such high stakes as the one about young Moses. What he learned in his early years in his parents' home was the basis for his future decisions to identify with his people and lead them out when God called. His head was not ultimately turned by the wealth and power of Egypt. He decided to share the reproach of the suffering and considered it precious.

Lord, I want all children to have that kind of basis for decisions. Use me today to teach those under my influence what they need. Amen.

THE MODEL PARENT

"If his sons forsake My law and do not walk in My judgments, if they break My statutes and do not keep My commandments, then I will punish their transgression with the rod, and their iniquity with stripes. Nevertheless My lovingkindness I will not utterly take from him, nor allow My faithfulnes to fail. My covenant I will not break, nor alter the word that has gone out of My lips."

PSALM 89:30–34 NKJV

O Lord, thank You that Your Word addresses everything we really need to know. You even gave us an example of good parenting as You interacted with Your children, Israel, throughout the Old Testament. In what I read today, You acknowledge that even if Your children sin against You, You will not withdraw Your love and covenant, though You will discipline severely. You mention the rod and stripes. These speak not of easy discipline but of painful consequences. Still, when the discipline is over, You will not forget Your promises or Your obligation. You want them to learn what they did wrong and return to Your embrace. Help me to be an example like that. Amen.

JUST DUST

*He has not dealt with us according to our sins,
nor punished us according to our iniquities. For as
the heavens are high above the earth, so great is
His mercy toward those who fear Him; as far as the
east is from the west, so far has He removed our
transgressions from us. As a father pities his children,
so the LORD pities those who fear Him. For He knows
our frame; He remembers that we are dust.*

PSALM 103:10–14 NKJV

Dear Lord, I'm thankful today that You don't hold my immaturity and frailty against me. Like a good Father, You take into account the fact that I have much to learn. When I first came to You for salvation, You didn't hold me off because of my sins. You listened to my confession and pulled me close into Your family. You gave me a heritage and paid my debt out of Your grace. And now You are preparing a home in heaven for me, where I can live forever with You! Thank You, Jesus! Amen.

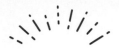

CHILDREN ARE GOD'S HERITAGE

Unless the LORD builds the house, they labor in vain who build it; unless the LORD guards the city, the watchman stays awake in vain.... Behold, children are a heritage from the LORD, the fruit of the womb is a reward. Like arrows in the hand of a warrior, so are the children of one's youth. Happy is the man who has his quiver full of them.

PSALM 127:1, 3–5 NKJV

Father God, thank You for creating the family and children. You could have set in place a pattern of replicating adult humans, but You chose to give us babies whom we could raise into adults. Too often, as earthly societies, we have not valued children as we should. In the past, terrible child labor occurred in factories. And today child abuse is rampant, not to mention the millions of children whose lives have been taken in the womb through abortion.

But Your Word tells us that these little ones are Your heritage and are meant to be the continuation of a father's faithful teaching. Thank You for providing the best model of this truth. Amen.

PARENTS WHO GIVE

"For everyone who asks receives, and the one who seeks finds, and to the one who knocks it will be opened. Or which one of you, if his son asks him for bread, will give him a stone? Or if he asks for a fish, will give him a serpent? If you then, who are evil, know how to give good gifts to your children, how much more will your Father who is in heaven give good things to those who ask him!"

MATTHEW 7:8–11 ESV

Dear Lord, thank You for the good things You give me. You are the perfect Father. You don't give me what is bad for me, although You don't always explain why bad things happen. I wouldn't understand if You did. But You do operate from a heart of perfect love for me; and as I learn to trust Your heart, I draw closer to You when I'm disappointed or frustrated or confused. I know I can trust that You are working out all things according to Your sovereign will. Amen.

THE FATHER'S KINGDOM

For you know how, like a father with his children, we exhorted each one of you and encouraged you and charged you to walk in a manner worthy of God, who calls you into his own kingdom and glory. And we also thank God constantly for this, that when you received the word of God, which you heard from us, you accepted it not as the word of men but as what it really is, the word of God, which is at work in you believers.

1 THESSALONIANS 2:11–13 ESV

. . . .

Father, here on earth, we are often identified by our family characteristics and name. Each family has some kind of reputation: an expectation of manner or behavior from those who know the parents. And our parents expect us to reflect them in a worthy manner.

Lord God, You want us to walk in the light and follow Your rules as loving family members. You have given us Your Word and Your Spirit and Your promise for the future. It is up to us to use these advantages and become children who make You happy. Please help us, Father. Amen.

DON'T SACRIFICE YOUR CHILDREN

They sacrificed their sons and their daughters to the demons; they poured out innocent blood, the blood of their sons and daughters, whom they sacrificed to the idols of Canaan, and the land was polluted with blood.... Save us, O LORD our God, and gather us from among the nations, that we may give thanks to your holy name and glory in your praise. Blessed be the LORD, the God of Israel, from everlasting to everlasting! And let all the people say, "Amen!" Praise the LORD!

PSALM 106:37–38, 47–48 ESV

Father God, Your people in the Old Testament were so influenced by the pagan nations around them that they actually adopted their horrifying practice of offering their children to the heathen gods of Canaan. In effect, they were giving over their children to the work of demons.

Today, Lord, we may not place our children in the scalding hands of a metal idol or throw them into the river for the crocodile god, but often we are careless in managing the precious gifts you've given us. And tragically, many children are sacrificed to the god of convenience in an abortion clinic. Forgive us and guide us back to You. Amen.

GLAD PARENTS

Hear, my son, and be wise, and direct your heart in the way. Be not among drunkards or among gluttonous eaters of meat, for the drunkard and the glutton will come to poverty, and slumber will clothe them with rags. Listen to your father who gave you life, and do not despise your mother when she is old. Buy truth, and do not sell it; buy wisdom, instruction, and understanding. The father of the righteous will greatly rejoice; he who fathers a wise son will be glad in him. Let your father and mother be glad; let her who bore you rejoice.

PROVERBS 23:19–25 ESV

Thank You, Lord, for my parents. They did their best to raise me right. Sure, they made mistakes, but I know they're human just like me. Help me remember to honor them even now by spending time with them when I can and by really listening when they talk to me. I want to make them glad just as I hope my children would want to do the same. Being a parent myself has helped me learn so much about Your Father's heart for me. I love You, Lord. Amen.

LOVE MEANS DISCIPLINE

He who loves wisdom makes his father glad.... The
rod and reproof give wisdom, but a child left to himself
brings shame to his mother.... Discipline your son, and
he will give you rest; he will give delight to your heart.

PROVERBS 29:3, 15, 17 ESV

• •

Father God, Your Word tells me that You discipline me
because You love me. If You didn't care, You wouldn't take
the trouble to reach out and correct me. Thank You that
You care so much. The psalmist David wrote about find-
ing comfort in the rod and staff. These tools were sometimes used for correction—but such discipline brings
security to a child, because the parent is a solid and
unmoving wall and the consequences of wrong behavior
are clear. Lord, I bring to You my parenting today. If I need
to have my attitude adjusted or my outlook renewed,
help me to understand that before it becomes a problem
that must be corrected. Thank You for being a good
Father. Amen.

A Mind Set on Prayer

A PURPOSEFUL PRAYER

Hear a just cause, O LORD; attend to my cry! Give ear to my prayer from lips free of deceit! From your presence let my vindication come! Let your eyes behold the right! You have tried my heart, you have visited me by night, you have tested me, and you will find nothing; I have purposed that my mouth will not transgress. With regard to the works of man, by the word of your lips I have avoided the ways of the violent. My steps have held fast to your paths; my feet have not slipped.

PSALM 17:1–5 ESV

Dear Lord, I'm so glad I can call out to You today with confidence that You will hear me. Thank You for testing me and examining my heart. Like the psalmist, I ask You to behold my heart, my actions, and my attitudes and see if there is anything wicked in me. Please show me where I need to correct wrong thinking about doctrine or relationships or discipleship. I lift this prayer to You right now, knowing that You hear me and will help me as I put my trust in You. Amen.

REST THROUGH PRAYER

Listen to my prayer, O God, and hide not Yourself from my supplication! Attend to me and answer me; I am restless and distraught in my complaint and must moan [and I am distracted] at the noise of the enemy, because of the oppression and threats of the wicked; for they would cast trouble upon me, and in wrath they persecute me. My heart is grievously pained within me, and the terrors of death have fallen upon me. Fear and trembling have come upon me; horror and fright have overwhelmed me. And I say, Oh, that I had wings like a dove! I would fly away and be at rest.

PSALM 55:1–6 AMPC

· ·

Sometimes, Lord, I come to You with my delights. Today I bring my distresses. I don't think my life is quite as fearful and chaotic as the psalmist's, but I feel overwhelmed right now. I ask that You would help me find soul rest in You, even though I can't fly away like the dove! Lord, show me the way out and help me to trust in You. Amen.

OUR CONFIDENCE

*Praise is awaiting You, O God, in Zion; and to You
the vow shall be performed. O You who hear prayer,
to You all flesh will come. Iniquities prevail against me;
as for our transgressions, You will provide atonement
for them. Blessed is the man You choose, and cause
to approach You, that he may dwell in Your courts.
We shall be satisfied with the goodness of Your
house, of Your holy temple. By awesome deeds
in righteousness You will answer us, O God of
our salvation, You who are the confidence of all
the ends of the earth, and of the far-off seas.*

PSALM 65:1–5 NKJV

Dear Lord, it is morning, and like the rest of creation, I look
to You for strength and nourishment for my day. Thank
You for being the confidence of all You have created.
We know that You will provide for us, and we thank You.
Our praise rises to You. Draw Your people ever closer to
You so that we may live in the light of Your love. Amen.

YOU HAVE HEARD ME!

Come and hear, all you who fear God, and I will declare what He has done for my soul. I cried to Him with my mouth, and He was extolled with my tongue. If I regard iniquity in my heart, the Lord will not hear. But certainly God has heard me; He has attended to the voice of my prayer. Blessed be God, who has not turned away my prayer, nor His mercy from me!

PSALM 66:16–20 NKJV

O God of all, I want to begin my prayer today by giving You all my praise. You have heard me! Though I'm just a speck here on planet earth—light-years from Your throne and not important in any way except by my designation as Your child—You hear me and listen intently when I pray.

Lord, I know Your close attention to me is conditional, because Your Word says if I harbor sin in my heart, You won't listen to me. I can't expect a holy God to help a heart that is rebellious. Help me to stay centered and humble. In Jesus' name. Amen.

DELIVER ME, LORD

But as for me, my prayer is to You, O Lord, in the acceptable time; O God, in the multitude of Your mercy, hear me in the truth of Your salvation. Deliver me out of the mire, and let me not sink; let me be delivered from those who hate me, and out of the deep waters. Let not the floodwater overflow me, nor let the deep swallow me up; and let not the pit shut its mouth on me.

PSALM 69:13–15 NKJV

Heavenly Father, today I come to You with problems that I can't solve. I need Your intervention in my situation. I ask You to hear me and deliver me and pull me out of the pit of trouble.

Lord, there are times when animals get stuck in the mud and can't get out. The farmer will put out brush and wood until a firm path is formed and the animal can walk out on the path provided. That's what I ask from You today. I need to learn from this pit, so please don't just pull me out, Lord; give me a corrected path to walk on. And then help me not to get caught in this situation again. Thank You! Amen.

GRACE CLOSES THE DISTANCE

*For the LORD shall build up Zion; He shall appear in His
glory. He shall regard the prayer of the destitute, and
shall not despise their prayer. This will be written
for the generation to come, that a people yet to be
created may praise the LORD. For He looked down
from the height of His sanctuary; from heaven the
LORD viewed the earth, to hear the groaning of the
prisoner, to release those appointed to death.*

PSALM 102:16–20 NKJV

Lord, there is so much sky between You and me. You dwell
in the heavens; I live on earth. Yet there is little distance
between Your love and me, because grace cannot be
measured in human miles. Thank You for looking down
out of Your heaven today. I ask that You would regard
my prayer and release me from the anxiety plaguing my
spirit. Lately I've struggled to keep a good attitude and
to believe that a brighter day is coming. But I trust in You
to bring it to pass. Amen.

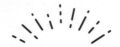

HE WATCHES AND HEARS

The eyes of the LORD are in every place, keeping watch on the evil and the good. A wholesome tongue is a tree of life, but perverseness in it breaks the spirit.... The sacrifice of the wicked is an abomination to the LORD, but the prayer of the upright is His delight. The way of the wicked is an abomination to the LORD, but He loves him who follows righteousness.

PROVERBS 15:3–4, 8–9 NKJV

. . . .

Dear Father, there is no place I can hide from You. And I don't want to. I want You to have open access to my heart and life. Your eyes can see everything, and Your ears can hear it all. You know if I'm living in righteousness or dabbling in the ways of the wicked. I want You to remind me that if I start toward a temptation in my heart, You know about it. Convict me, Lord, by Your Holy Spirit and show me the path of escape.

I don't want to do what is an abomination in Your sight. Instead, I want to delight myself in what is pure and holy. In Jesus' name. Amen.

ACCEPTING CORRECTION

The LORD is far from the wicked, but He hears the prayer of the righteous. The light of the eyes rejoices the heart, and a good report makes the bones healthy. The ear that hears the rebukes of life will abide among the wise. He who disdains instruction despises his own soul, but he who heeds rebuke gets understanding. The fear of the LORD is the instruction of wisdom, and before honor is humility.

PROVERBS 15:29–33 NKJV

Lord God, my reading today tells me that if I resist instruction, I hate my own soul! I don't want that to be true of me, yet I admit I have a hard time accepting correction. Please help me to know the difference between instruction and humiliation. Lord, there are times I just need to listen to what my best friend is telling me instead of overreacting to it as though she is putting me down. There are things she knows that I don't, and I need her to tell me. Give me confidence in my spirit so I can deal with healthy conflict and become a better person for it.

I want to have wisdom, and so I want to have a healthy fear of You. Show me how to live in a spirit of humility. Amen.

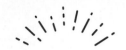

THE RIGHT ATTITUDE

Better is the poor who walks in his integrity than one perverse in his ways, though he be rich. Whoever keeps the law is a discerning son, but a companion of gluttons shames his father. One who increases his possessions by usury and extortion gathers it for him who will pity the poor. One who turns away his ear from hearing the law, even his prayer is an abomination.

PROVERBS 28:6–9 NKJV

Dear Father, I ask You today to examine my attitude toward others. I understand that how I think in my heart about those around me affects how I approach Your throne. If I'm haughty and proud and self-sufficient, I won't receive anything from You. I don't want my prayer to be an abomination. I want to come before You with a humble, teachable spirit.

When Jesus walked this earth, He said we should approach the throne of God as a child, believing and expectant, vulnerable and real. That's how I want to come today. In Jesus' name. Amen.

ALL PEOPLES

For thus says the Lord: To the eunuchs who keep My Sabbaths and choose the things which please Me and hold firmly My covenant—to them I will give in My house and within My walls a memorial and a name better [and more enduring] than sons and daughters; I will give them an everlasting name that will not be cut off.... All these I will bring to My holy mountain and make them joyful in My house of prayer. Their burnt offerings and their sacrifices will be accepted on My altar; for My house will be called a house of prayer for all peoples.

Isaiah 56:4–5, 7 AMPC

Lord God, in my Bible reading today, I am so intrigued by the fact that You spoke specifically about eunuchs—those who were forcibly made infertile for one reason or another. In times of war, sometimes young men were forced into service for another king who didn't want any threats to his throne from palace workers, and so they were castrated. In any case, Lord, You specifically mentioned them and said You would give them a better legacy than having sons or daughters if they would hold to Your covenant. Thank You for being a just and compassionate God. Your house is for *all* people. Amen.

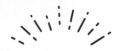

THE PRAYER OF JONAH

The waters compassed me about, even to [the extinction of] life; the abyss surrounded me, the seaweed was wrapped about my head. I went down to the bottoms and the very roots of the mountains; the earth with its bars closed behind me forever. Yet You have brought up my life from the pit and corruption, O Lord my God. When my soul fainted upon me [crushing me], I earnestly and seriously remembered the Lord; and my prayer came to You, into Your holy temple.

JONAH 2:5-7 AMPC

Dear God, I can't imagine what it would be like to pray to You from the inside of a whale's belly. I can't imagine the terror; I can't imagine the stench. I can't imagine the despair at believing this would be the way I would die. But You hadn't lost track of Jonah, the prophet who was running from You. You heard his prayer of repentance, and You gave him another chance.

Thank You, Lord, for hearing me in my terrifying places. Help me always to obey and avoid that kind of prayer place! Amen.

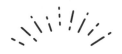

REVIVE YOUR WORK

A prayer of Habakkuk the prophet, set to wild, enthusiastic, and triumphal music. O Lord, I have heard the report of You and was afraid. O Lord, revive Your work in the midst of the years, in the midst of the years make [Yourself] known! In wrath [earnestly] remember love, pity, and mercy. God [approaching from Sinai] came from Teman [which represents Edom] and the Holy One from Mount Paran [in the Sinai region]. Selah [pause, and calmly think of that]! His glory covered the heavens and the earth was full of His praise. And His brightness was like the sunlight; rays streamed from His hand, and there [in the sunlike splendor] was the hiding place of His power.

HABAKKUK 3:1–4 AMPC

- -

O Lord, I need reviving in my spirit. And so do many of my friends and family. We trust You and want to serve You, but today we need Your refreshing power to rest on us. Your glory covers the heavens, and the earth is full of Your praise. Your brightness is more brilliant than the sun. I ask, like the prophet, that You would remember Your love and pity and mercy toward us. I lift my spirit to You this day. In the name of Jesus. Amen.

CONTINUAL PRAYER

[Let your] love be sincere (a real thing); hate what is evil [loathe all ungodliness, turn in horror from wickedness], but hold fast to that which is good. Love one another with brotherly affection [as members of one family], giving precedence and showing honor to one another. Never lag in zeal and in earnest endeavor; be aglow and burning with the Spirit, serving the Lord. Rejoice and exult in hope; be steadfast and patient in suffering and tribulation; be constant in prayer.

ROMANS 12:9–12 AMPC

Lord Jesus, I want my life today to be a reflection of the life You lived. These verses from Romans give me some spiritual goals to accomplish every day. You, the perfect Son of God, always lived this way. Please empower me so that I can live in my best imitation of the way You did. You are the Master Teacher; I want to be a good student. May my spirit always be set to the "on" prayer position. I can't actually pray out loud every minute, but I can have my heart attuned to You at all times. Amen.

ALL MANNER OF PRAYER

*Lift up over all the [covering] shield of saving faith,
upon which you can quench all the flaming missiles
of the wicked [one]. And take the helmet of salvation
and the sword that the Spirit wields, which is the
Word of God. Pray at all times (on every occasion, in
every season) in the Spirit, with all [manner of] prayer
and entreaty. To that end keep alert and watch with
strong purpose and perseverance, interceding in
behalf of all the saints (God's consecrated people).*

EPHESIANS 6:16–18 AMPC

Dear Lord, when I don't properly equip myself for the day,
I can be putting myself in danger as I face Satan's attacks.
Help me today to don all the spiritual armor You have
provided and to use it well in those battle moments. Part
of my defense is prayer, both for myself and for others.
I thank You that I don't even have to remember all the
names of those I'm praying for. And that's a good thing,
because sometimes I forget. But You know the thoughts
and intents of my heart. And You can work accordingly in
the lives of those I bring to Your throne. Amen.

PRAYER FOR A QUIET LIFE

First of all, then, I admonish and urge that petitions,
prayers, intercessions, and thanksgivings be offered on
behalf of all men, for kings and all who are in positions
of authority or high responsibility, that [outwardly] we
may pass a quiet and undisturbed life [and inwardly]
a peaceable one in all godliness and reverence and
seriousness in every way. For such [praying] is good
and right, and [it is] pleasing and acceptable to God
our Savior, Who wishes all men to be saved and
[increasingly] to perceive and recognize and discern
and know precisely and correctly the [divine] Truth.

1 TIMOTHY 2:1–4 AMPC

Lord God, You have commanded us in Your Word to pray
for those in authority. And so I do. And there is a reward
for this kind of prayer—when the rulers are fair minded
and just, we are able to live quiet, godly lives. You want
all people to be saved, and You will work out Your will,
no matter what happens on earth. But it is good for us to
pray for those who rule over us so that we may be part
of a chain of people living in harmonious and peaceful
community. Thank You, Lord, for Your gifts in my life. Amen.

PRAYERS OF POWER

Confess to one another therefore your faults (your slips, your false steps, your offenses, your sins) and pray [also] for one another, that you may be healed and restored [to a spiritual tone of mind and heart]. The earnest (heartfelt, continued) prayer of a righteous man makes tremendous power available [dynamic in its working].

JAMES 5:16 AMPC

Dear Lord, some days I need to pray for healing for my body. And other days I need to pray for healing in my spirit. You care about both. And if I pray from a basis of righteousness in You, my prayers will have great power.

I'm reminded of the stories in the Bible of those who prayed for healing. Lord, You know whether healing or suffering will best glorify Your name. I ask that You would give me a humble, submissive spirit so that whichever way You choose to answer my prayer, I will fully surrender to Your plan. I pray in Jesus' name. Amen.

PRAYERS IN GOLDEN BOWLS

He then went and took the scroll from the right hand of Him Who sat on the throne. And when He had taken the scroll, the four living creatures and the twenty-four elders [of the heavenly Sanhedrin] prostrated themselves before the Lamb. Each was holding a harp (lute or guitar), and they had golden bowls full of incense (fragrant spices and gums for burning), which are the prayers of God's people (the saints). And [now] they sing a new song, saying, You are worthy to take the scroll and to break the seals that are on it, for You were slain (sacrificed), and with Your blood You purchased men unto God from every tribe and language and people and nation.

REVELATION 5:7–9 AMPC

Lord Jesus, You are worthy to receive my praise today. Thank You for being the One worthy to open the heavenly scrolls and redeem mankind. Your perfect worthiness makes my heart happy today.

I read today about the prayers of the saints stored up in golden bowls. They smell fragrant to You, like incense. Thank You for treasuring my prayers; they come from the deepest part of me. I rest in the knowledge that You hear them and value them. Amen.

I AM HEARD

*And this is the confidence (the assurance,
the privilege of boldness) which we have in Him:
[we are sure] that if we ask anything (make any
request) according to His will (in agreement with His
own plan), He listens to and hears us. And if (since) we
[positively] know that He listens to us in whatever
we ask, we also know [with settled and absolute
knowledge] that we have [granted us as our present
possessions] the requests made of Him.*

1 JOHN 5:14–15 AMPC

Dear Lord God, often I have doubts about my significance to others. It can be so easy to believe that my needs and feelings are not important when compared to the needs and feelings of others. But I know I can come to You without hesitation, believing You care about every detail of my life. These verses tell me that if I'm asking for Your help to live my life in Your will, I can be confident in knowing You hear me. Thank You for hearing me today. Amen.

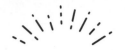

A PRAYER OF WEEPING

*I am weary with my groaning; all night I soak my
pillow with tears, I drench my couch with my weeping.
My eye grows dim because of grief; it grows old
because of all my enemies. Depart from me, all
you workers of iniquity, for the Lord has heard
the voice of my weeping. The Lord has heard my
supplication; the Lord receives my prayer.*

PSALM 6:6–9 AMPC

Dear Father, sometimes I don't come to You with a happy heart; I come to You with a heavy heart and tears. I want to have a positive outlook every day, but You know that life is filled with ups and downs, and bad times do come. I've had nights when I cried into my pillow until I fell asleep; and I've had days when nothing in my world seemed right. Now and then, I might just be having one of those hormonal days when everything looks bleak; while other times, a real tragedy has occurred in my life or in the life of someone I love. In these difficult times, I can't act like nothing is wrong.

Today, Lord, I ask that You would hold me while I grieve and give me grace to face this difficulty. Let me dig deep into Your strength and rest in Your comfort. In Jesus' name. Amen.

YOUR WORD IS GOOD

Let my mournful cry and supplication come [near] before You, O Lord; give me understanding (discernment and comprehension) according to Your word [of assurance and promise]. Let my supplication come before You; deliver me according to Your word! My lips shall pour forth praise [with thanksgiving and renewed trust] when You teach me Your statutes. My tongue shall sing [praise for the fulfillment] of Your word, for all Your commandments are righteous.

PSALM 119:169–172 AMPC

Father in heaven, today I am very thankful for Your Word. It teaches me how to live; it shows me where I need to improve; it reminds me of Your faithfulness; it gives me hope in my trials; and it helps me focus on what really matters—eternity with You.

I want to live with an attitude of thanksgiving as I recall all the reasons I have to be joyful in You and in Your Word. Thank You for preserving it for me down through the generations of time. I believe it is Your holy and infallible truth, and I will treasure it. Amen.

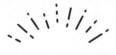

IN YOUR PRESENCE

I said to the Lord, You are my God; give ear to the voice of my supplications, O Lord. O God the Lord, the Strength of my salvation, You have covered my head in the day of battle.... I know and rest in confidence upon it that the Lord will maintain the cause of the afflicted, and will secure justice for the poor and needy [of His believing children]. Surely the [uncompromisingly] righteous shall give thanks to Your name; the upright shall dwell in Your presence (before Your very face).

Psalm 140:6–7, 12–13 ampc

Lord God, this morning as I get up and start my day, I'm grateful I can live it in Your presence. You have been my strength in the days when I have felt the heat of spiritual battle. You are a righteous advocate for those who are poor and needy. And I know You will be with me today, just as You have always been with me. I go forth today in that settled hope. Amen.

PERFECT GOODNESS

Listen to my words, O Lord, give heed to my sighing and groaning. Hear the sound of my cry, my King and my God, for to You do I pray. In the morning You hear my voice, O Lord; in the morning I prepare [a prayer, a sacrifice] for You and watch and wait [for You to speak to my heart]. For You are not a God Who takes pleasure in wickedness; neither will the evil [man] so much as dwell [temporarily] with You. Boasters can have no standing in Your sight; You abhor all evildoers.

PSALM 5:1–5 AMPC

Father God, may my prayer come before You today as a fragrant sacrifice to Your perfect goodness. I cherish Your uncompromising holiness and praise You because no evil can be found in You. You are the Righteous One, and You can never have part in evil. Because of Your goodness, I know I can trust Your plans for me. You could never be prejudiced or careless or vengeful. Everything that comes to me from You comes through a heart of pure holiness and love. Thank You, Lord! Amen.

A Mind Set on Promises

A STRENGTH AND SHIELD

To You I will cry, O LORD my Rock: do not be silent to me, lest, if You are silent to me, I become like those who go down to the pit. Hear the voice of my supplications when I cry to You, when I lift up my hands toward Your holy sanctuary. . . . Blessed be the LORD, because He has heard the voice of my supplications! The LORD is my strength and my shield; my heart trusted in Him, and I am helped; therefore my heart greatly rejoices, and with my song I will praise Him.

PSALM 28:1–2, 6–7 NKJV

Lord God, I bless Your name this day as I wait before You in prayer, lifting my hands toward Your holy sanctuary. You are strong when I am weak. You are a shield when I am unprotected. You are a song when I don't have a melody. I ask that You not be silent but instead speak into the stillness of this morning as I wait for You. As I go about the duties and responsibilities of my life this day, I want to be aware of the plan You have for me. In Jesus' name. Amen.

A NEW SONG

I waited patiently for the LORD; and He inclined to me, and heard my cry. He also brought me up out of a horrible pit, out of the miry clay, and set my feet upon a rock, and established my steps. He has put a new song in my mouth—praise to our God; many will see it and fear, and will trust in the LORD.

PSALM 40:1–3 NKJV

Good morning, Lord! You are the song I sing today. You rescued me from the pit of sin. You gave my feet a secure place to stand. You show me the path forward so I can take confident steps. You hear me when I call to You. I rejoice in Your care and goodness.

Lord, I've always been a little in awe of those who engage in serious rock climbing. They inch their way up what look like impossible ascents. In my spiritual life, You have helped me to be a rock climber. You took me from the bottom to where I am today. And I know You will be the strength that takes me all the way to the peak. Thank You, Lord! Amen.

A SHELTER

Hear my cry, O God; attend to my prayer. From the end of the earth I will cry to You, when my heart is overwhelmed; lead me to the rock that is higher than I. For You have been a shelter for me, a strong tower from the enemy. I will abide in Your tabernacle forever; I will trust in the shelter of Your wings. Selah. For You, O God, have heard my vows; You have given me the heritage of those who fear Your name.

PSALM 61:1–5 NKJV

Dear heavenly Father, I'm grateful today as I lift this prayer to You. Whenever I face a situation that seems like too much for me, I can turn to You. Your tabernacle, Your presence with me, is the center of my hope. When I feel overwhelmed by the cares and injustices and trials of my world, I can run into the shelter of Your wings like a little chick runs to its mother in a storm. You have given me a heritage forever in Your family. And nothing can happen to me that would prevent You from being a tower of strength for me. I stand amazed at Your grace and goodness. And today, right now, I praise You because You are my God. Amen.

I AM YOUR SERVANT

Bow down Your ear, O LORD, hear me; for I am poor and needy. Preserve my life, for I am holy; You are my God; save Your servant who trusts in You! Be merciful to me, O Lord, for I cry to You all day long. Rejoice the soul of Your servant, for to You, O Lord, I lift up my soul. For You, Lord, are good, and ready to forgive, and abundant in mercy to all those who call upon You. Give ear, O LORD, to my prayer; and attend to the voice of my supplications. In the day of my trouble I will call upon You, for You will answer me.

PSALM 86:1–7 NKJV

· ·

Father God, today I affirm that I am Your servant, ready to do Your will. I need to remember that I have a place in Your great household of faith. I am Your child, yet I am also a servant in the respect that I acknowledge You as my Lord and Master. Thank You for being good and ready to forgive and abundant in mercy. I know that You hear me when I call and that You will answer me. Thank You for being my God. Amen.

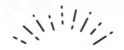

PRAYING FOR THE PROMISE

*Then He said to them, "Thus it is written,
and thus it was necessary for the Christ to
suffer and to rise from the dead the third day,
and that repentance and remission of sins should
be preached in His name to all nations, beginning
at Jerusalem. And you are witnesses of these
things. Behold, I send the Promise of My Father
upon you; but tarry in the city of Jerusalem until
you are endued with power from on high."*

LUKE 24:46–49 NKJV

Dear God, I didn't have the privilege of living in the time when Jesus walked our earth. You planned for me to be alive now, in this day, and I trust Your goodness. But if I had been alive then, I would have wanted to be part of the group of disciples waiting in that upper room for the fulfillment of Your promise—the blessing of the Holy Spirit. Today I ask that You would empower me to be a witness for You. I can't do it in my own strength, but I can in Yours. Show me if there is anything in my life that is hindering the Spirit's indwelling, and make me a vessel You can use. Amen.

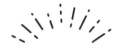

AN UNWAVERING FAITH

He did not waver at the promise of God through unbelief, but was strengthened in faith, giving glory to God, and being fully convinced that what He had promised He was also able to perform. And therefore "it was accounted to him for righteousness." Now it was not written for his sake alone that it was imputed to him, but also for us. It shall be imputed to us who believe in Him who raised up Jesus our Lord from the dead, who was delivered up because of our offenses, and was raised because of our justification.

ROMANS 4:20–25 NKJV

Lord, today as I pray, I'm thinking about Abraham and his faith in You. He was strengthened to keep believing that You would fulfill Your promise, and it was credited to him as righteousness. You, Lord, see our faith as true evidence of Your work in us, for You are the One who gives us faith to begin with. Abraham didn't waver or stagger at the audacious possibility that he would have a son. And in Your perfect timing, You brought it to pass. I believe You for the seemingly impossible things in my life too. In Jesus' name. Amen.

THE BEST GUARANTEE

We who first trusted in Christ should be to the praise of His glory. In Him you also trusted, after you heard the word of truth, the gospel of your salvation; in whom also, having believed, you were sealed with the Holy Spirit of promise, who is the guarantee of our inheritance until the redemption of the purchased possession, to the praise of His glory.

EPHESIANS 1:12–14 NKJV

. . . .

Lord Jesus, when You left this earth, You promised to send the Comforter, the Holy Spirit. And You did. On the Day of Pentecost, the Holy Spirit came in fullness and power, transforming the lives of the believers in that upper room and empowering them to become the world-changing force You used to spread the Gospel.

Not only is the Holy Spirit our means of spiritual energy and power, but He is also the living guarantee or proof of our sonship and daughtership. Because we are sealed with His presence in our lives, we know that we are truly in Your family. I am so grateful for the reality of my spiritual adoption. Thank You, Lord, for making a place for me. Amen.

ENDURING FAITH AND A CROWN OF LIFE

For no sooner has the sun risen with a burning heat than it withers the grass; its flower falls, and its beautiful appearance perishes. So the rich man also will fade away in his pursuits. Blessed is the man who endures temptation; for when he has been approved, he will receive the crown of life which the Lord has promised to those who love Him.

JAMES 1:11–12 NKJV

Father God, today the sun is shining somewhere, even if it's not blazing brilliantly on me. Because of the way You created our universe, the sun continues to bring warmth and enable life on our earth even when it seems chilly and cloudy outside. Out in space, in the place where you set it, the sun is doing its job faithfully, continually.

But just as too much sunshine can wither plants, so those who set their sights only on this earth and its wealth will dry up and blow away. Only those who withstand the temptation to focus exclusively on this life will be given the crown of life someday. Lord, I want to be in that number. Amen.

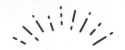

PRECIOUS PROMISES

*May you know more and more of grace and peace
as your knowledge of God and Jesus our Lord grows
deeper. He has by his own action given us everything
that is necessary for living the truly good life, in allowing
us to know the one who has called us to him, through
his own glorious goodness. It is through him that God's
greatest and most precious promises have become
available to us men, making it possible for you to
escape the inevitable disintegration that lust produces
in the world and to share in God's essential nature.*

2 PETER 1:2–4 PHILLIPS

Lord Jesus, I am so thankful for the promises in Your Word. You have given us, by Your grace, everything we need to live this life to which You call us. We have endless grace and peace available to us through Your riches. We have the hope of eternity with You. And we have the knowledge that You are preserving us in the midst of the disintegration going on in the culture around us.

As I grow and mature in my faith, I realize how blessed I am to have security in You. Nothing can truly shake me when I stand fast in the assurance that You will never leave me. Amen.

ETERNAL LIFE—
THE BEST PROMISE

Therefore let that abide in you which you heard from the beginning. If what you heard from the beginning abides in you, you also will abide in the Son and in the Father. And this is the promise that He has promised us— eternal life. . . . And now, little children, abide in Him, that when He appears, we may have confidence and not be ashamed before Him at His coming. If you know that He is righteous, you know that everyone who practices righteousness is born of Him.

1 JOHN 2:24–25, 28–29 NKJV

. . . .

O God in heaven, You called me Your child the instant I trusted You for salvation. You have prepared me for righteous works in Your name. You have given me confidence in my purpose in You. And You have given me the ultimate promise—life unending in Your presence.

When I experience the sadness and pain and tragedy and distortion of this earth, I am so grateful for this abiding comfort in my heart. Nothing I face here on earth can take away the future I have with You. Amen.

PRESERVED

My help comes from the LORD, who made heaven and earth. He will not allow your foot to be moved; He who keeps you will not slumber. Behold, He who keeps Israel shall neither slumber nor sleep. The LORD is your keeper; the LORD is your shade at your right hand. The sun shall not strike you by day, nor the moon by night. The LORD shall preserve you from all evil; He shall preserve your soul.

PSALM 121:2–7 NKJV

Dear Father, some days I just need to be reminded that I am not alone and that You are constantly watching over me. I am so glad You are never tired and never fall asleep. Your eyes are always on me. Whether I'm experiencing the heat of the afternoon sun or the lonely rays of the moon at night, You are there. You shield me from the blast and hold me when I'm afraid. You preserve my soul from the evil one. And I can rest assured that my steps are secure in You. Amen.

IT SHALL COME TO PASS

Trust in the LORD, and do good; dwell in the land, and feed on His faithfulness. Delight yourself also in the LORD, and He shall give you the desires of your heart. Commit your way to the LORD, trust also in Him, and He shall bring it to pass. He shall bring forth your righteousness as the light, and your justice as the noonday.

PSALM 37:3–6 NKJV

. . . .

Lord God, I pray about and think about so many things throughout my day. When I get up in the morning and face my reflection in the mirror, I think about the things happening in my life and in the lives of those I love. I think about the fact that I'm getting older and things are changing around me. I think about my family members and my responsibilities to them. I think about my work and my pleasure and my debts and my challenges. And I am reminded today in these verses that I can commit all of these things to You. You want me to find my ultimate delight in You and trust You with the other aspects of life. You will bring forth righteousness in me and bring to pass whatever is good and right and fulfills Your purpose. Amen.

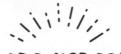

A PROMISE FOR
THOSE WHO CARE

Blessed is he who considers the poor; the LORD will deliver him in time of trouble. The LORD will preserve him and keep him alive, and he will be blessed on the earth; You will not deliver him to the will of his enemies. The LORD will strengthen him on his bed of illness; You will sustain him on his sickbed.

PSALM 41:1–3 NKJV

. . . .

Dear Lord, when You walked the earth, You were far from wealthy. You didn't enjoy a luxurious home or the comfort of an easy life. You chose to belong to the working class and to identify with the common man. You wanted everyone to feel comfortable coming to You. And You welcomed anyone and everyone.

You tell me in Your Word to have consideration for the poor. You bless those who have hearts of compassion. You promise to strengthen and sustain them. There are times when I have struggled financially, and so I understand some of the fears and frustrations. Help me always to be a friend to those in need. In Jesus' name. Amen.

LIGHT AND REJOICING

*You who love the LORD, hate evil! He preserves
the souls of His saints; He delivers them out
of the hand of the wicked. Light is sown for the
righteous, and gladness for the upright in heart.
Rejoice in the LORD, you righteous, and give
thanks at the remembrance of His holy name.*

PSALM 97:10–12 NKJV

. . . .

Dear Father God, I love the light! In my earthly life, the
light of morning gives me hope as I start another day.
When the days grow darker in the winter months, I miss
the warming rays of the sun. The seasons remind me of
how blessed I am to have You as the light of my soul. You
are always shining for me. You do not dwell in darkness,
and You abhor evil. You have promised to deliver Your
people from the hands of the wicked one. Satan can't get
to me to harm my soul.

Today, as I go out from my place of prayer to interact
with others, I ask that You would clothe me with Your light
and love so that I may be a beacon of hope to others. The
world is shrouded in darkness, but Your light always wins.
Thank You for the light! Amen.

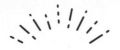

GUARDED BY UNDERSTANDING

For the LORD gives wisdom; from his mouth come knowledge and understanding; he stores up sound wisdom for the upright; he is a shield to those who walk in integrity, guarding the paths of justice and watching over the way of his saints. Then you will understand righteousness and justice and equity, every good path; for wisdom will come into your heart, and knowledge will be pleasant to your soul; discretion will watch over you, understanding will guard you.

PROVERBS 2:6–11 ESV

Dear Lord, I don't know much about the shields used in ancient times, but I understand that they kept the user from danger. You have promised to be a shield for me and to guard the path of justice. Honesty and fair dealings and uprightness matter to You, Lord. You watch over Your saints, and You want us to reflect Your values and Your ways of interacting with others.

Thank You for revealing the way to wisdom and discretion and understanding. I want to use what You have given me, so that I can have a heart of love toward others and a heart of integrity toward You. Amen.

MY STRONGHOLD

I love you, O LORD, my strength. The LORD is my rock and my fortress and my deliverer, my God, my rock, in whom I take refuge, my shield, and the horn of my salvation, my stronghold. I call upon the LORD, who is worthy to be praised, and I am saved from my enemies. The cords of death encompassed me; the torrents of destruction assailed me; the cords of Sheol entangled me; the snares of death confronted me. In my distress I called upon the LORD; to my God I cried for help. From his temple he heard my voice, and my cry to him reached his ears.

PSALM 18:1–6 ESV

• •

Dear Lord, You are worthy to be praised. You hear my voice when I call to You. You are my fortress of strength and my refuge, a stronghold, a place entirely secure from any breach by the enemy. When I am frightened by the uncertainties of life, I can hide my soul in the Rock. Yes, I will still face hard things; but I will face them with the certainty that nothing can happen to me in this life that the next one will not heal. I love You, Lord. You are my God. Amen.

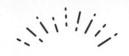

TAKE COURAGE!

The LORD is my light and my salvation; whom shall I fear? The LORD is the stronghold of my life; of whom shall I be afraid?... For he will hide me in his shelter in the day of trouble; he will conceal me under the cover of his tent; he will lift me high upon a rock.... I believe that I shall look upon the goodness of the LORD in the land of the living! Wait for the LORD; be strong, and let your heart take courage; wait for the LORD!

PSALM 27:1, 5, 13–14 ESV

. . . .

Lord God, deep in my heart, I hold fast to Your goodness. I believe You are working out all things for the good of those who trust in You. You have a mighty purpose, and I am a part of it today and every day. Show me how I fit into what You are doing on this earth. Thank You that I don't have to fear anyone today, because You are my light and salvation. Though I grow impatient in my desire to see good things come to pass, I will wait for You. Though there is trouble around me, I will take courage in Your name. I will be strong in Your strength. Amen.

SOLID GROUND

God is our refuge and strength, a very present help in trouble. Therefore we will not fear though the earth gives way, though the mountains be moved into the heart of the sea, though its waters roar and foam, though the mountains tremble at its swelling. There is a river whose streams make glad the city of God, the holy habitation of the Most High. God is in the midst of her; she shall not be moved; God will help her when morning dawns.

PSALM 46:1–5 ESV

Lord of All, when an earthquake comes and the very mountains seem to be trembling on their foundations, You are solid ground. There are times in my life when nothing seems firm, but I know I can stand in You. Though I feel flooded with sorrow and trouble, You are unmoved. I'm so grateful to know that You have built for me a future city with a river that never overflows its banks but that makes the inhabitants happy. Someday I will live there, far removed from the cares and concerns of this temporal world. I put my trust in You today and look forward to that future reality. Amen.

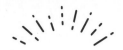

YOU ARE WHAT I DESIRE

*Nevertheless, I am continually with you; you hold
my right hand. You guide me with your counsel, and
afterward you will receive me to glory. Whom have I in
heaven but you? And there is nothing on earth that I
desire besides you. My flesh and my heart may fail, but
God is the strength of my heart and my portion forever.
For behold, those who are far from you shall perish;
you put an end to everyone who is unfaithful to you.
But for me it is good to be near God; I have made the
Lord GOD my refuge, that I may tell of all your works.*

PSALM 73:23–28 ESV

O Father, when my strength is flagging, You are my portion forever. When my spirit is feeling low, You hold me up. You guide me with Your counsel and someday will receive me into the glories of Your heaven.

Nothing I might desire on earth can compare with the joy I've discovered in living in relationship with You. Though my heart may fail, You lend me Your supernatural strength. It is good for me to be near You. You are my constant refuge, Lord. I will tell of all Your works! Amen.

BLESSED MORE THAN THE BIRDS

*Even the sparrow finds a home, and the swallow
a nest for herself, where she may lay her young,
at your altars, O LORD of hosts, my King and my God.
Blessed are those who dwell in your house, ever
singing your praise! Blessed are those whose strength
is in you, in whose heart are the highways to Zion.*

PSALM 84:3–5 ESV

· ·

Dear Father God, You are the One who upholds all creation. You care about the creatures of the field and sky and sea because You made them. You created them to inhabit this planet and bring life and presence and comfort. Jesus used the birds of the air as illustrations in His teachings. He reminded us that You feed the birds and that You see whenever a sparrow falls to the ground. The Old Testament speaks of Your people having strength like the mighty pinions of an eagle and soaring in Your power.

But we as Your human creations are even more blessed than the animals. We have minds to reason and understand. And we see Your hand as You care for us, even more than for the birds. Thank You! Amen.

WE ARE YOUR PEOPLE

For the LORD is a great God, and a great King above all gods. In his hand are the depths of the earth; the heights of the mountains are his also. The sea is his, for he made it, and his hands formed the dry land. Oh come, let us worship and bow down; let us kneel before the LORD, our Maker! For he is our God, and we are the people of his pasture, and the sheep of his hand.

PSALM 95:3–7 ESV

Creator God, You are a great King. You rule the heavens and the earth. You formed everything that is in existence. Your hands are big enough to hold the mass of the earth, and Your stature is taller than the peaks of the great mountains. You fashioned the seas and shaped the dry land. Everything is Yours, and everything has been made for Your glory.

This morning, I bow down before You in recognition of Your greatness. You are my God. You have made us to be the people of Your pasture—meaning You care for us as a shepherd, lovingly feeding us and leading us. I am so thankful to be Yours! Amen.

A Mind Set above Pain

THE RUTHLESS STORM

*O Lord, you are my God; I will exalt you; I will praise
your name, for you have done wonderful things, plans
formed of old, faithful and sure. . . . For you have been
a stronghold to the poor, a stronghold to the needy in
his distress, a shelter from the storm and a shade from
the heat; for the breath of the ruthless is like a storm
against a wall, like heat in a dry place. You subdue
the noise of the foreigners; as heat by the shade of
a cloud, so the song of the ruthless is put down.*

ISAIAH 25:1, 4–5 ESV

Father God, there are times when I face the pain of living
on this cursed earth. Bad things happen to those around
me and to me too. I know that You have unshakable plans
for good and that those plans will come to pass. Because
I'm assured of Your goodness, I hold to You in my times of
distress. There is no tragedy or suffering or sorrow that
You cannot enable me to endure. I praise Your name for
this truth. Amen.

THE LIFE OF JESUS IN ME

But we have this treasure in jars of clay, to show that the surpassing power belongs to God and not to us. We are afflicted in every way, but not crushed; perplexed, but not driven to despair; persecuted, but not forsaken; struck down, but not destroyed; always carrying in the body the death of Jesus, so that the life of Jesus may also be manifested in our bodies. For we who live are always being given over to death for Jesus' sake, so that the life of Jesus also may be manifested in our mortal flesh.

2 CORINTHIANS 4:7–11 ESV

Lord Jesus, when you were on earth, You shared in my humanity. The Bible tells me You were subjected to the same types of pain and sorrow that I face. You know what little aches and pains are like, and You also know the depth of extreme agony. You experienced the sting of betrayal when Your friends abandoned You in Your hardest moments. You know what it feels like to be lied about and falsely accused. You know about loneliness and grief. But You were victorious; and because of that, I can be too! My life in this body is like a precious treasure held in a fragile pot. But You sustain me every day. Amen.

CONTENT WITH WEAKNESSES

*But he said to me, "My grace is sufficient for you,
for my power is made perfect in weakness."
Therefore I will boast all the more gladly of my
weaknesses, so that the power of Christ may rest
upon me. For the sake of Christ, then, I am content
with weaknesses, insults, hardships, persecutions,
and calamities. For when I am weak, then I am strong.*

2 Corinthians 12:9–10 esv

Dear Father, I don't like to be weak. I love when I awaken in the morning to a feeling of vigor and strength. I like to feel refreshed and ready for the day, unhindered by my frailties and inabilities.

I know that every human being deals with some type of suffering, some type of inadequacy. As much as we may appear to have no problems, we still struggle in hidden ways. All of us need another Source of strength at some point in our lives. Thank You for being my power when I am weak. Thank You for carrying me when I can't make it on my own stamina. I face weakness in this physical body, but You never fail me. Amen.

A DIFFERENT PERSPECTIVE

In my opinion whatever we may have to go through now is less than nothing compared with the magnificent future God has planned for us. The whole creation is on tiptoe to see the wonderful sight of the sons of God coming into their own. The world of creation cannot as yet see reality, not because it chooses to be blind, but because in God's purpose it has been so limited—yet it has been given hope. And the hope is that in the end the whole of created life will be rescued from the tyranny of change and decay, and have its share in that magnificent liberty which can only belong to the children of God!

ROMANS 8:18–21 PHILLIPS

. . . .

Dear Lord, when I look into Your Word, I am reminded that the eternal perspective is different from the earthly perspective. When I look at my present suffering in light of the eternal weight of glory, I can see that there is no comparison. All of creation is groaning now under the curse of sin, but one day the curse will be no more, for there will be a new heaven and a new earth for us. Amen.

ENDURANCE IN THE LORD

For our example of the patient endurance of suffering we can take the prophets who have spoken in the Lord's name. Remember that it is usually those who have patiently endured to whom we accord the word "blessed!" You have heard of Job's patient endurance and how God dealt with him in the end, and therefore you have seen that the Lord is merciful and full of understanding pity for us men.

JAMES 5:10–11 PHILLIPS

. . . .

Lord God, many of Your prophets suffered greatly. The Old Testament is filled with stories of those who endured great trials and sorrows. Often when we think of great calamity, we think of Job. And that is fitting, because few have gone through what he endured. Losing his family and his possessions and his health all in one afternoon can only be called catastrophic. And yet he was enabled, by Your strength, to endure without losing his grip on Your faithfulness. He trusted You despite his circumstances. His story, and the stories of others who have endured, help me to hang on to You when I struggle. I know You are merciful and full of compassion, and I thank You for Your goodness today. Amen.

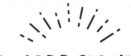

NO MORE SIGHING

*And a highway shall be there, and a way; and it shall
be called the Holy Way. The unclean shall not pass
over it, but it shall be for the redeemed; the wayfaring
men, yes, the simple ones and fools, shall not err
in it and lose their way. No lion shall be there, nor
shall any ravenous beast come up on it; they shall
not be found there. But the redeemed shall walk
on it. And the ransomed of the Lord shall return
and come to Zion with singing, and everlasting joy
shall be upon their heads; they shall obtain joy and
gladness, and sorrow and sighing shall flee away.*

ISAIAH 35:8–10 AMPC

Lord Jesus, I look forward to the day when Your eternal
kingdom will come and all will be made new. When I read
about it now, it seems so far away and so foreign to my
earthly understanding. It's like reading about a science
fiction world because it is so different from my present
world. Down here, we have much to sigh about; but in
Your coming kingdom, sorrow and sighing will flee away!
Thank You for that hope! Amen.

LIFE-GIVING WORDS

*And I will delight myself in Your commandments,
which I love. My hands also I will lift up to Your
commandments, which I love, and I will meditate on
Your statutes. Remember the word to Your servant,
upon which You have caused me to hope. This is my
comfort in my affliction, for Your word has given me life.*

PSALM 119:47–50 NKJV

Lord God, when I'm in the middle of a troubling and painful time, I often find comfort in the words of others. Even if they cannot take away the pain I am experiencing, their acknowledgment of my hurt and their reassurance of Your love give me strength.

Lord, as I delight myself in You and learn Your Word, I'm able to meditate on Your goodness and Your words of hope and promise when I'm troubled. Your words give me such consolation in my dark times; they are actually life-giving! They are not mere symbols on a page but are the power of Your character put into human communication. I am so grateful for the delight I have in You. Amen.

HEALING FOR THE BROKENHEARTED

And He was handed the book of the prophet Isaiah. And when He had opened the book, He found the place where it was written: "The Spirit of the LORD is upon Me, because He has anointed Me to preach the gospel to the poor; He has sent Me to heal the brokenhearted, to proclaim liberty to the captives and recovery of sight to the blind, to set at liberty those who are oppressed; to proclaim the acceptable year of the LORD."

LUKE 4:17–19 NKJV

. . . .

Lord Jesus, I am so thankful You came to our earth to heal the brokenhearted. The curse of sin and its effects have left so many people broken in body and soul. You came as the fulfillment of the Father's promise to redeem the human condition. What You did on the cross marked the end of the reign of sin; Satan is defeated. Though the earth is not yet made new, You have begun the work in the souls of those who trust in You. You promise deliverance to those held captive and liberty to those suffering oppression by the enemy. I bring my pain to You today, knowing You will draw me close and heal my hurting heart. Amen.

DELIVERANCE FROM AFFLICTION

The righteous cry out, and the LORD hears, and delivers them out of all their troubles. The LORD is near to those who have a broken heart, and saves such as have a contrite spirit. Many are the afflictions of the righteous, but the LORD delivers him out of them all.... The LORD redeems the soul of His servants, and none of those who trust in Him shall be condemned.

PSALM 34:17–19, 22 NKJV

Father God, this morning as I bring my day to You, I'm glad I know You hear me when I cry out to You. You see everything that happens to me and save me from my trouble. Because I trust in You, I know I won't be condemned but will have Your hope and life.

There are no human answers for the terrible suffering that takes place on our planet, but there are eternal answers. Someday I will have a better understanding; though I will never be able to comprehend Your matchless wisdom, which is so much greater than my own. You are the source of all righteousness. I trust You and Your holy character. Amen.

A Mind Set on Pleasing God

LOVE THE LORD YOUR GOD

"Therefore you shall love the LORD your God, and keep His charge, His statutes, His judgments, and His commandments always. Know today that I do not speak with your children, who have not known and who have not seen the chastening of the LORD your God, His greatness and His mighty hand and His outstretched arm.... Therefore you shall keep every commandment which I command you today, that you may be strong, and go in and possess the land which you cross over to possess, and that you may prolong your days in the land which the LORD swore to give your fathers, to them and their descendants, 'a land flowing with milk and honey.'"

DEUTERONOMY 11:1–2, 8–9 NKJV

Father in heaven, You planned from before time that Your people would live in covenant with You. You gave us commands and spoke to us through Your prophets and Your Word and then through Your Son. While we are not saved by works, we show our love for You by our works. If we truly love You, we want to please You in all we do. I pray that You will help me today to be diligent in honoring Your commands. Amen.

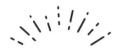

CHOOSE TO HONOR AND OBEY

"I call heaven and earth as witnesses today against you,
that I have set before you life and death, blessing
and cursing; therefore choose life, that both you
and your descendants may live; that you may love
the LORD your God, that you may obey His voice,
and that you may cling to Him, for He is your life
and the length of your days; and that you may dwell
in the land which the LORD swore to your fathers,
to Abraham, Isaac, and Jacob, to give them."

DEUTERONOMY 30:19–20 NKJV

Lord God, just as You did for the people of old, You have
set before me the choice of life or death. If I choose to obey
Your commands, I will experience life. But if I choose my
own way, then I am actually choosing death because there
is no life outside of relationship with You. You are my life
and the length of my days. I want to dwell with You forever,
and so I must honor what You tell me in Your Word. You
made promises to Abraham, Isaac, and Jacob and followed
through to fulfill them. I know I can trust You too. Amen.

REJECT REBELLION AND STUBBORNNESS

So Samuel said: "Has the LORD as great delight in burnt offerings and sacrifices, as in obeying the voice of the LORD? Behold, to obey is better than sacrifice, and to heed than the fat of rams. For rebellion is as the sin of witchcraft, and stubbornness is as iniquity and idolatry. Because you have rejected the word of the LORD, He also has rejected you from being king."

1 SAMUEL 15:22–23 NKJV

Dear Lord, the stories in the Bible instruct me and warn me. When I read this account of how King Saul did what he thought was best instead of following the clear directions of the Lord, I am reminded that I must not become careless in my obedience to You. Witchcraft is a serious sin against You, and I don't want to be associated with it. I don't want to have a stubborn heart that leads me into idolatry. I don't want to be rejected by You, and so I will reject these tendencies to sin and ask You to give me a pliable, teachable heart that follows after You. Amen.

OBEY THOSE IN GODLY AUTHORITY

Every word of God is pure; He is a shield to those
who put their trust in Him. Do not add to His words,
lest He rebuke you, and you be found a liar. . . . The
eye that mocks his father, and scorns obedience
to his mother, the ravens of the valley will pick
it out, and the young eagles will eat it.

PROVERBS 30:5–6, 17 NKJV

. . . .

Lord God, nothing can be added to Your Word. It is pure
and whole, just as You gave it. I cannot know truth outside
of You, for I am subject to error. But You know exactly what
is right and true. You tell me in Your Word to honor those
You've placed in authority over me—and that began with
my parents. Lord, some parents are more in touch than
others, and some don't even try very hard; but You have
called me to honor their position and never to mock or
make fun. Even in the way I refer to them, I want to show
deference and kindness. These verses use strong words
showing just how seriously You look at this matter. With
Your help, I will please You by honoring my parents. Amen.

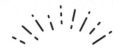

WALK IN OBEDIENCE

"Who among you fears the Lord? Who obeys the voice of His Servant? Who walks in darkness and has no light? Let him trust in the name of the Lord and rely upon his God. Look, all you who kindle a fire, who encircle yourselves with sparks: walk in the light of your fire and in the sparks you have kindled."

Isaiah 50:10–11 NKJV

. . . .

Heavenly Father, I want to have a healthy respect for You and Your commands. I want to please You today by the way I live. I want to trust in Your name and rely on You for strength.

The words of Your prophets were sometimes dismissed by the people who heard them. I don't want to fall into that kind of sin. I want to put You on the throne of my heart so that I will keep Your ways always before me. I want to walk in the light of Your holy fire so that the sparks that fall around me will kindle a flame in others. Amen.

OBEY GOD, NOT MEN

*But Peter and the other apostles answered
and said: "We ought to obey God rather than men.
The God of our fathers raised up Jesus whom you
murdered by hanging on a tree. Him God has exalted
to His right hand to be Prince and Savior, to give
repentance to Israel and forgiveness of sins. And we
are His witnesses to these things, and so also is the Holy
Spirit whom God has given to those who obey Him."*

ACTS 5:29–32 NKJV

• •

Dear God, Your will is that I respect the authority You have put on earth. You have established earthly rulers so that justice and order might prevail. But anytime the ruling authorities command me to do something that violates Your will, I must do as the apostles and make the choice to obey You first.

The Old Testament prophet Daniel did this when he continued to pray three times a day despite the decree outlawing it. And You took care of him. I know You will guide and care for me when I have to make this kind of choice someday. Amen.

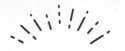

SERVE THE CAUSE
OF RIGHTEOUSNESS

*Thank God that you, who were at one time
the servants of sin, honestly responded to the
impact of Christ's teaching when you came under
its influence. Then, released from the service of sin,
you entered the service of righteousness. (I use
an everyday illustration because human nature
grasps truth more readily that way.) In the past you
voluntarily gave your bodies to the service of vice and
wickedness—for the purpose of becoming wicked. So,
now, give yourselves to the service of righteousness—
for the purpose of becoming really good.*

<small>ROMANS 6:17–20 PHILLIPS</small>

O Lord, when I lived in sin, I didn't realize that I was a slave. I thought I was having a good time. But after You opened my eyes to the truth, I saw that I was really living in service to Satan, doing things that were destructive to me and to others, giving myself over to wickedness. Now I want to serve You with a pure passion. I want the motivations of my heart to be set on righteousness. I thank You that You have changed my heart and my desires. In Jesus' name. Amen.

LOVE EACH OTHER

Now that you have, by obeying the truth, made your souls clean enough for a genuine love of your fellows, see that you do love each other, fervently and from the heart. For you are the sons of God now; the live, permanent Word of the living God has given you his own indestructible heredity. It is true that: "All flesh is as grass, and all the glory of man as the flower of the grass. The grass withers, and its flower falls away, but the word of the Lord endures for ever".

1 PETER 1:22–25 PHILLIPS

- -

Lord Jesus, because I have surrendered my life to You, I want to obey the truth. I am Your child, and as a child of the Most High God, I want my behavior to reflect Your values and principles. All other goals are as fleeting as the grass or the flowers that spring forth and then die.

As I obey the truth of Your Word, I must have a genuine love for my fellow believers. You want me to love You by loving them—this is the great law of love You've given us. Help me to fulfill it today. Amen.

BEAR FRUIT

We also pray that your outward lives, which men see, may bring credit to your master's name, and that you may bring joy to his heart by bearing genuine Christian fruit, and that your knowledge of God may grow yet deeper. As you live this new life, we pray that you will be strengthened from God's boundless resources, so that you will find yourselves able to pass through any experience and endure it with courage. You will even be able to thank God in the midst of pain and distress because you are privileged to share the lot of those who are living in the light.

<small>COLOSSIANS 1:9–12 PHILLIPS</small>

Today, O Lord, I commit to living my outward life in such a way that I will have fruit to show. The only way I can bear fruit is by staying connected to You, the life-giving Source. Only then will I have the spiritual strength to flourish. I can go through any experience with courage if I am rooted deeply in You. Thank You for giving me the grace to endure hard times and to live in love with those around me. Amen.

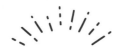

AIM TO PLEASE GOD

Our message to you is true, our motives are pure, our conduct is absolutely above board. We speak under the solemn sense of being trusted by God with the Gospel. We do not aim to please men, but to please God who knows us through and through.... And so we are continually thankful that when you heard us preach the word of God you accepted it, not as a mere human message, but as it really is, God's Word, a power in the lives of you who believe.

1 Thessalonians 2:3–4, 13 Phillips

Lord God, You know me through and through. You have given me the Holy Spirit to teach me how to live. You have given me human teachers and preachers who share with me what You have shown them. Thank You for these avenues of learning that increase my knowledge of You and Your ways. Since I want to live my life in a manner pleasing to You, I need these sources of wisdom. Help me never to resist teaching that comes from You. Let me look into Your Word as I listen; and if I find that Your truth is being taught, let me accept it with my whole heart and learn from it. Amen.

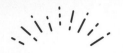

TRUST AND OBEY

And if, dear friends of mine, when we realise this our hearts no longer accuse us, we may have the utmost confidence in God's presence. We receive whatever we ask for, because we are obeying his orders and following his plans. His orders are that we should put our trust in the name of his Son, Jesus Christ, and love one another—as we used to hear him say in person. The man who does obey God's commands lives in God and God lives in him, and the guarantee of his presence within us is the Spirit he has given us.

1 JOHN 3:21–24 PHILLIPS

Almighty Father, thank You for the gift of Your Son. Because of His work on the cross, I can have confidence in Your presence; I can have the guarantee of Your life in me through the Holy Spirit.

When I have a heart of obedience and submission to You, my heart doesn't accuse me and I have peace. Full surrender to You is the best way to live. When I follow Your plan, I can pray in Your will and receive the answers I need. When pleasing You is my goal, I know that I live in You, close to Your heart and with Your blessing. Amen.

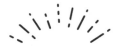

OBEDIENCE—
THE RIGHT SACRIFICE

But know that the LORD has set apart the godly
for himself; the LORD hears when I call to him....
Offer right sacrifices, and put your trust in the
LORD. There are many who say, "Who will show us
some good? Lift up the light of your face upon us,
O LORD!" You have put more joy in my heart than
they have when their grain and wine abound.

PSALM 4:3, 5–7 ESV

O Lord, as I look into Your Word and do my best to follow Your principles, I know that obedience is the right kind of sacrifice. In the Old Testament, sacrifices of animals and grain were required because Jesus had not yet died. There were different types of offerings for different types of spiritual needs. Your people were to offer You their very best, not what was left over or the diseased or defective. I'm so grateful I can offer You the sacrifice that pleases You—the gift of my submitted will and my devoted love. I will gladly put my trust in You and offer the sacrifice of my obedience today. I love You, Lord. Amen.

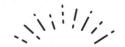

ANSWER THE QUESTIONS

O LORD, who shall sojourn in your tent? Who shall dwell on your holy hill? He who walks blamelessly and does what is right and speaks truth in his heart; who does not slander with his tongue and does no evil to his neighbor, nor takes up a reproach against his friend.

PSALM 15:1–3 ESV

• •

Lord God, You care about the details of my obedience to You. These verses penned by the psalmist are not a nonchalant inquiry. Only those who are serious about their relationship with You will receive Your blessings. You don't want me to use my tongue in sinful ways or to treat others unkindly. You want me to do what is right and to speak truth. I commit to living a life of integrity so that I can enjoy closeness with You. Just as healthy earthly relationships require me to care about the desires of others, my eternal relationship with You requires me to focus on pleasing You. Help me to love and serve You wholeheartedly, Lord! Amen.

OUR RIGHTEOUS LORD

The LORD is in his holy temple; the LORD's
throne is in heaven; his eyes see, his eyelids test
the children of man. The LORD tests the righteous,
but his soul hates the wicked and the one who loves
violence. Let him rain coals on the wicked; fire and
sulfur and a scorching wind shall be the portion
of their cup. For the LORD is righteous; he loves
righteous deeds; the upright shall behold his face.

PSALM 11:4–7 ESV

Holy Father God, I'm grateful You love righteousness. If You were not completely righteous, I couldn't put my trust in You, for You might not be completely trustworthy. But I know You will always do what is right. And You expect me to live a life of righteousness too. You test me to see if I am truly committed to serving You. You look over the earth for those who will commit themselves to integrity and honor and obedience. Someday You will punish the evildoers who refused Your ways and disdained the death of Your Son. Thank You that I can escape that judgment because of Christ! I pray in His name. Amen.

THE JUDGE OF THE EARTH

*Let the heavens be glad, and let the earth rejoice;
let the sea roar, and all that fills it; let the field exult,
and everything in it! Then shall all the trees of the
forest sing for joy before the Lord, for he comes, for
he comes to judge the earth. He will judge the world
in righteousness, and the peoples in his faithfulness.*

Psalm 96:11–13 esv

Dear Lord, someday the earth will sing as You come to judge the earth and make all things new. You will set everything right and put the scales of justice in perfect balance. You have perfect knowledge of all the inhabitants of the earth, and You will make the perfect judgments about us and our actions and our faith. On that day, I want to be found in You, having listened to Your voice and obeyed Your commands. I know that, because I have received salvation in Him, Jesus will be my advocate. His shed blood is my only hope of entering eternal joy in heaven. Today I ask You to be my guide and open my eyes to the paths of righteousness so that I can be found in You on that day. Amen.

THE GLORY OF HIS RIGHTEOUSNESS

*Clouds and thick darkness are all around him;
righteousness and justice are the foundation of
his throne. Fire goes before him and burns up his
adversaries all around. His lightnings light up the
world; the earth sees and trembles. The mountains
melt like wax before the LORD, before the Lord
of all the earth. The heavens proclaim his
righteousness, and all the peoples see his glory.*

PSALM 97:2–6 ESV

O Lord, the very earth is aware of Your righteousness. Though this planet groans under the curse of sin, it still responds to Your voice. You have set the times and seasons in place; they operate on the cycle You created. You have determined the rising of the tides and the blooming of seeds and the gestational growth of preborn babies—and they respond to Your plan. The laws of gravity and weather patterns are very much in place. You control this old world, even in its degenerate state. The mountains would melt like wax before You if You did not uphold them. Everything around me recognizes Your holiness. I will join in that song today. Amen.

THE BLESSEDNESS OF RIGHTEOUSNESS

Praise the LORD! Oh give thanks to the LORD, for he is good, for his steadfast love endures forever! Who can utter the mighty deeds of the LORD, or declare all his praise? Blessed are they who observe justice, who do righteousness at all times! ... Blessed be the LORD, the God of Israel, from everlasting to everlasting! And let all the people say, "Amen!" Praise the LORD!

PSALM 106:1–3, 48 ESV

Dear Father, I am at peace in Your righteousness today. I know that those who live in obedience to Your laws are blessed. There is no way to declare all the wonderful things You have done, but today I want to be part of the chorus of praise to You. You are good, and Your love is faithful and unchanging. The people of God should say "Amen" and sing praises to You for Your goodness!

When I recall how faithful You have been to me, I am amazed. From my childhood to today, You have been reaching out to me, showing me Your care and inviting me to know You in a personal way. Thank You for Your righteous love, Lord! Amen.

RIGHTEOUSNESS BRINGS LIFE

The hand of the diligent will rule, while the slothful will be put to forced labor. Anxiety in a man's heart weighs him down, but a good word makes him glad. One who is righteous is a guide to his neighbor, but the way of the wicked leads them astray. Whoever is slothful will not roast his game, but the diligent man will get precious wealth. In the path of righteousness is life, and in its pathway there is no death.

PROVERBS 12:24–28 ESV

Lord, You give us many practical principles in Your Word, all of them based on the righteousness of Your character. You want us to be diligent and not slothful, because You Yourself are diligent and have created us in Your image. In the path of righteousness, there is no spiritual death; and someday it will lead to both physical and spiritual life for all eternity.

I want my life to be hidden with You so that You receive the glory for whatever good I do. As I trust You to accomplish Your will in my life, I know that You and Your perfect character will be cause for rejoicing. I commit to following Your righteous path for my life. In Jesus' name. Amen.

AN ESTABLISHED THRONE

When a man's ways please the LORD, he makes even his enemies to be at peace with him. Better is a little with righteousness than great revenues with injustice. The heart of man plans his way, but the LORD establishes his steps. An oracle is on the lips of a king; his mouth does not sin in judgment. A just balance and scales are the LORD's; all the weights in the bag are his work. It is an abomination to kings to do evil, for the throne is established by righteousness.

PROVERBS 16:7–12 ESV

Dear God, I know that You rule over all. You set up those whom You will and remove them as You see fit. And though we make many plans, You are the One who establishes what will happen in our lives.

I read in the Bible about the kings of Israel; some of them were righteous, and some were not. Some caused the people they ruled to fall into great sin against You. King David is remembered as a strong leader, but even he sinned against You and suffered the consequences in his children. The only King who always does right is You, and someday You will reign over all. In the meantime, help me to follow You with my whole heart. Amen.

THE PURSUIT OF RIGHTEOUSNESS

*Whoever pursues righteousness and kindness
will find life, righteousness, and honor. A wise man
scales the city of the mighty and brings down the
stronghold in which they trust. Whoever keeps his
mouth and his tongue keeps himself out of trouble. . . .
No wisdom, no understanding, no counsel can avail
against the LORD. The horse is made ready for the
day of battle, but the victory belongs to the LORD.*

PROVERBS 21:21–23, 30–31 ESV

Dear Father God, I know I will face the battle of temptation today. Satan is always seeking to throw before me some new way to please myself outside of Your will. As a result, I need to pursue righteousness with abandon. No wisdom or understanding that I could seek is more effective than just spending time with You and Your Word. Like a horse is made ready for battle, I want my mind to be ready for the day. Victory belongs to You, and You will let me share in it if I ask in Jesus' name. Amen.

RIGHTEOUSNESS AND PRAISE WILL SPROUT

For I the LORD love justice; I hate robbery and wrong.... I will greatly rejoice in the LORD; my soul shall exult in my God, for he has clothed me with the garments of salvation; he has covered me with the robe of righteousness, as a bridegroom decks himself like a priest with a beautiful headdress, and as a bride adorns herself with her jewels. For as the earth brings forth its sprouts, and as a garden causes what is sown in it to sprout up, so the Lord GOD will cause righteousness and praise to sprout up before all the nations.

ISAIAH 61:8, 10–11 ESV

Dear Lord, in today's reading, You tell us that You love what is right and hate what is wrong. And You want us to share in Your righteousness and be clothed, as it were, in the garments of salvation. My soul can be beautifully cloaked in Your holiness so that I will bring glory to You. And as the earth in the garden brings forth the life of the seeds that are sown, so You will cause holy and righteous traits to sprout up from the life You plant in me. I will rejoice today in Your provision for me and in Your holy name. Amen.

NO CONDEMNATION FOR THE RIGHTEOUS

There is therefore now no condemnation for those who are in Christ Jesus. For the law of the Spirit of life has set you free in Christ Jesus from the law of sin and death. For God has done what the law, weakened by the flesh, could not do. By sending his own Son in the likeness of sinful flesh and for sin, he condemned sin in the flesh, in order that the righteous requirement of the law might be fulfilled in us, who walk not according to the flesh but according to the Spirit.

ROMANS 8:1–4 ESV

. . . .

O Lord, as I meditate on the words You have given us in Your Word, I am blessed to know that Your righteousness can be fulfilled in me—if I walk according to the leading of Your Spirit. There is no condemnation for me now that I have been set free from the ways of sin through Jesus' sacrifice for me. You made a way for me to partake of Your holiness, and there is no better way to live. Today I lift up my plans and goals to You and ask that You would be glorified in me as I walk in obedience to You. Amen.

RENEWED TO LIVE IN HIS LIKENESS

But that is not the way you learned Christ!—assuming that you have heard about him and were taught in him, as the truth is in Jesus, to put off your old self, which belongs to your former manner of life and is corrupt through deceitful desires, and to be renewed in the spirit of your minds, and to put on the new self, created after the likeness of God in true righteousness and holiness.

EPHESIANS 4:20–24 ESV

Heavenly Father, thank You for teaching me Your way through so many means. You have put people in my life who have shown me what discipleship is all about. You have let me discover the truth about Jesus and how I can put off what is sinful and put on what is good. I don't have to walk in the deceitful desires I once knew. I can be renewed in my mind and reflect the likeness of God in true righteousness.

Thank You for renewing me in Your image. You created man and woman long ago to be Your image-bearers. Sin has marred our reflection of You. But in Jesus, we are renewed to wholeness. Amen.

THE SEED OF RIGHTEOUSNESS

*No one who abides in him keeps on sinning; no one
who keeps on sinning has either seen him or known
him. Little children, let no one deceive you. Whoever
practices righteousness is righteous, as he is righteous.
Whoever makes a practice of sinning is of the devil,
for the devil has been sinning from the beginning. The
reason the Son of God appeared was to destroy the
works of the devil. No one born of God makes a practice
of sinning, for God's seed abides in him; and he cannot
keep on sinning, because he has been born of God.*

1 John 3:6–9 esv

Father God, as I have learned more about You, I have
come to know that living in relationship with You is the
way to avoid sin. I want my actions and attitudes to
come from a heart that is committed to You. Please help
me to choose what is right and avoid what is wrong.
Jesus, You came to earth to destroy the works of the
devil, and You enable me to do what is right. I have the
seed of righteousness in me through Your Spirit, and it
will bring forth fruit. Thank You! Amen.

A Mind Set on Practical Christian Living

DEPART FROM EVIL

*Come, you children, listen to me; I will teach
you to revere and worshipfully fear the Lord.
What man is he who desires life and longs for many
days, that he may see good? Keep your tongue
from evil and your lips from speaking deceit.
Depart from evil and do good; seek, inquire for,
and crave peace and pursue (go after) it! The eyes
of the Lord are toward the [uncompromisingly]
righteous and His ears are open to their cry.*

PSALM 34:11–15 AMPC

Dear God, Your Word shows me how to please You in the practical aspects of my life. You have told me to be careful with my words and to stay away from evil. If I do these two things specifically, I will have a happier life. But more importantly, I will be doing what is right and what will bear eternal fruit. As I learn to revere and worshipfully fear You, Lord, You open Your ears to my cry and fill me with Your peace. Today, as I tackle my to-do list, help me to remember Your instruction. Amen.

SEVEN ABOMINABLE THINGS

These six things the Lord hates, indeed, seven are an abomination to Him: a proud look [the spirit that makes one overestimate himself and underestimate others], a lying tongue, and hands that shed innocent blood, a heart that manufactures wicked thoughts and plans, feet that are swift in running to evil, a false witness who breathes out lies [even under oath], and he who sows discord among his brethren.

PROVERBS 6:16–19 AMPC

Father God, I want to stay away from what grieves You. And You have given me a list of things to avoid. These violations of Your law are popular in culture today, but they are never popular with You. It doesn't matter who thinks otherwise when You have given Your will on a certain matter. Everyone else can be wrong, but You determine what is right.

Help me to live my life for You by recognizing the things You hate. When I know the boundaries, I can live in a healthy way without grieving Your heart. I pray in Jesus' name. Amen.

GODLY WISDOM

Be not envious of evil men, nor desire to be with them;
for their minds plot oppression and devise violence,
and their lips talk of causing trouble and vexation.
Through skillful and godly Wisdom is a house (a life,
a home, a family) built, and by understanding it is
established [on a sound and good foundation], and
by knowledge shall its chambers [of every area] be
filled with all precious and pleasant riches. A wise man
is strong and is better than a strong man, and a man
of knowledge increases and strengthens his power.

PROVERBS 24:1–5 AMPC

Lord, I need to operate on the basis of godly wisdom. When I do, I can see things clearly. I'm not envious of those who live wicked, but successful, lives. I can see that what they have today will not last. When I build my home on godly wisdom, it will have a good foundation and its rooms will be filled with pleasantness and joy. What's more, it is better for me to be wise than strong, because wisdom inevitably leads to power. Thank You for this practical advice from Your Word! Amen.

SLOW TO ANGER

Better is the end of a thing than the beginning of it,
and the patient in spirit is better than the proud in
spirit. Do not be quick in spirit to be angry or vexed,
for anger and vexation lodge in the bosom of fools.
Do not say, Why were the old days better than these?
For it is not wise or because of wisdom that you ask
this. Wisdom is as good as an inheritance, yes, more
excellent it is for those [the living] who see the sun.
For wisdom is a defense even as money is a defense,
but the excellency of knowledge is that wisdom
shields and preserves the life of him who has it.

ECCLESIASTES 7:8–12 AMPC

. . . .

Lord God, anger is a human emotion, a response to stimuli, a feeling evoked by injustice or irritation. *Feeling* anger is not necessarily wrong; how I manage it is what determines whether I am living in true holiness or mere selfishness. These verses instruct me to not be hasty in anger and to remember that only foolish people allow their anger to control them. And if I have this mindset, I will also grasp hold of the kind of wisdom that will enrich my life in other ways. Thank You, Lord, for teaching me through Your Word. Amen.

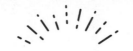

GENEROUS AND JUST

*It is well with the man who deals generously
and lends, who conducts his affairs with justice.
He will not be moved forever; the [uncompromisingly]
righteous (the upright, in right standing with God)
shall be in everlasting remembrance. He shall not be
afraid of evil tidings; his heart is firmly fixed, trusting
(leaning on and being confident) in the Lord. His heart
is established and steady, he will not be afraid while he
waits to see his desire established upon his adversaries.*

PSALM 112:5–8 AMPC

Lord God, You have said that it will be well with me if I am generous and just. This is just another example of the practicality of Your instruction to me. Now, of course, these traits might not always be rewarded here on earth. I think of Joseph, who was unjustly accused even though he was kind and just to others. But in the end, You caused him to triumph over those who wanted to bring him down. And You blessed his life and his influence. You will do the same for me if I put my trust in You. Amen.

HARMONIOUS LIVING

Live in harmony with one another; do not be haughty (snobbish, high-minded, exclusive), but readily adjust yourself to [people, things] and give yourselves to humble tasks. Never overestimate yourself or be wise in your own conceits. Repay no one evil for evil, but take thought for what is honest and proper and noble [aiming to be above reproach] in the sight of everyone.

ROMANS 12:16–17 AMPC

Father God, teach me today to love Your children—the ones who are easy to get along with *and* the ones who irritate me. You teach me not to be in contention with them but to strive for peace and unity. This instruction takes for granted that we won't all see things alike; for if we did, there would be no need for unity—we would be the same. But since we're not, I must remember to let You work in me a meek spirit and a willingness to do humble tasks. I must seek to promote the interests of others instead of catering to my own whims. Please give me grace to live in harmony with the people You've placed in my life. In Jesus' name. Amen.

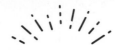

RICHES THROUGH HUMILITY

*A good name is to be chosen rather than great riches,
loving favor rather than silver and gold. The rich and
the poor have this in common, the LORD is the maker of
them all. A prudent man foresees evil and hides himself,
but the simple pass on and are punished. By humility
and the fear of the LORD are riches and honor and life.*

PROVERBS 22:1–4 NKJV

Dear Lord, You have given me a good name—*Your name.*
Because I have put my trust in Christ, I am known as a
Christian. This title was first used in ancient Antioch, and
it literally means "a little Christ." That definition is not
meant to be irreverent, but rather an indication that I am
a reflection of my Master. Since I have that name, I want
to live up to it well. And today's Bible reading reminds
me that when I practice humility and reverence for You,
I can have riches and honor and life. These riches are
not necessarily tangible, for many ungodly people also
have monetary wealth. Rather, these are spiritual riches
in Christ—available only to those who trust in Him. I'm so
grateful to belong to You, Lord! Amen.

SUBMISSION TO AUTHORITY

Likewise you younger people, submit yourselves to your elders. Yes, all of you be submissive to one another, and be clothed with humility, for "God resists the proud, but gives grace to the humble." Therefore humble yourselves under the mighty hand of God, that He may exalt you in due time, casting all your care upon Him, for He cares for you.

1 PETER 5:5–7 NKJV

Lord Jesus, when You came to earth, You humbled Yourself under the Father's will. You often said that You had come not to do Your own will, but to accomplish the will of Him who sent You. You modeled for me and all believers the shape of godly submission. When I humble myself as Your child, You enable me to live a life worthy of honor. In the church, I must submit to the elders—to those in spiritual authority. In the home, I must honor the structure You laid out for us. In society, I must have an appropriate spirit when I interact with those in civil authority. You care about every aspect of my daily life and give me apt instruction in Your Word. I am grateful! Amen.

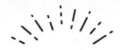

CAREFULLY CHOSEN FRIENDS

The hand of the diligent will rule, but the lazy man
will be put to forced labor. Anxiety in the heart of
man causes depression, but a good word makes it
glad. The righteous should choose his friends carefully,
for the way of the wicked leads them astray. The
lazy man does not roast what he took in hunting,
but diligence is man's precious possession.

PROVERBS 12:24–27 NKJV

. . . .

Dear Lord, the people I spend time with make a difference in my life. I can't be careless in deciding whom I want for friends. Thank You for speaking about the importance of good friends in Your Word. You didn't make us to be isolated but to live in community. Even at the dawn of creation, You said it wasn't good for the first man to be alone—You created Eve for him. And then You gave us families and neighbors and the Body of Christ. All of these avenues of relationship are important, and I want to develop them well.

Today, help me to be the kind of friend who is a good influence on those in my group. I don't want to be a negative force but rather enrich the lives of those in my circle of friends. Amen.

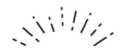

A FORGIVING SPIRIT

Therefore, as the elect of God, holy and beloved,
put on tender mercies, kindness, humility, meekness,
longsuffering; bearing with one another, and forgiving
one another, if anyone has a complaint against
another; even as Christ forgave you, so you
also must do. But above all these things put
on love, which is the bond of perfection.

COLOSSIANS 3:12–14 NKJV

Lord Jesus, You came to earth to show us the Father. When You taught us to forgive, You modeled for us what God the Father is like. He has great mercy in spite of our sin. Because He wasn't willing that any of us should perish, He planned a way of redemption. And You went all the way to the cross to finish the work. Now, as I live in relationship with others, I need to have a forgiving spirit. I must bear with others' faults and flaws and never hold them to a standard higher than that which I want for myself. And as I open my heart so You can fill me with Your mighty love, You tie together all the qualities of Christian character in a perfect bond. In Jesus' name. Amen.

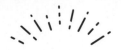

AN EXEMPLARY REFLECTION

*For to this end we both labor and suffer reproach,
because we trust in the living God, who is the Savior
of all men, especially of those who believe. These
things command and teach. Let no one despise your
youth, but be an example to the believers in word, in
conduct, in love, in spirit, in faith, in purity. Till I come,
give attention to reading, to exhortation, to doctrine.*

1 TIMOTHY 4:10–13 NKJV

Father in heaven, I come to You today needing Your grace to live this life to which You've called me. I want to be an exemplary reflection of Your life in me. I don't want to be a good example so I appear better than other believers, but rather because I have the responsibility to do my very best as Your child. Today, please help me in the following areas:

- My words—may they be filled with grace.
- My conduct—may it be tempered by the Holy Spirit's voice.
- My love—may it be the unifying force in my attitude.
- My spirit—may my joy in You be contagious.
- My faith—may I hold fast to my trust in You.
- My purity—may I never relinquish my integrity.

Thank You, Lord, for helping me in all the practical aspects of godliness. Amen.

BLAMELESS AND HARMLESS

For it is God who works in you both to will and to do for His good pleasure. Do all things without complaining and disputing, that you may become blameless and harmless, children of God without fault in the midst of a crooked and perverse generation, among whom you shine as lights in the world.

PHILIPPIANS 2:13–15 NKJV

Lord God, this passage sums up my prayers focused on practical Christian living. Basically, I need to be a light in a dark place. The power in me through Your Spirit is the exact opposite of the force at work in the world around me—the world controlled by Satan and his evil schemes. You call me to come against this darkness with my light. I am to celebrate my life in Christ and unashamedly let my influence be felt. Your Spirit directs me in holiness in every part of my daily life. Thank You for living Your life in me! Amen.

A Mind Set on Praise

GLORIOUS IN POWER

"The LORD is my strength and song, and He has become my salvation; He is my God, and I will praise Him; my father's God, and I will exalt Him.... Your right hand, O LORD, has become glorious in power; Your right hand, O LORD, has dashed the enemy in pieces.... Who is like You, O LORD, among the gods? Who is like You, glorious in holiness, fearful in praises, doing wonders?"

EXODUS 15:2, 6, 11 NKJV

Today, O Lord, as I pause to think about the day ahead of me, I remind myself that You are my strength and song. That means You are both my physical and my spiritual strength. I look to You for the grace I need for this day.

These verses in Exodus were sung to You after You delivered Your people from Pharaoh's army. You took an impossible situation for man and turned it into triumph. You do the same for me when I trust in You. You set me free from sin; You heal my wounds; You give me hope when I'm mired in despair. You are the God of wonders. I look to You today. Amen.

OUR SALVATION AND STRONGHOLD

"The LORD is my rock and my fortress and my deliverer;
the God of my strength, in whom I will trust; my shield
and the horn of my salvation, my stronghold and
my refuge; my Savior, You save me from violence.
I will call upon the LORD, who is worthy to be
praised; so shall I be saved from my enemies."

2 SAMUEL 22:2–4 NKJV

Dear Father, I recall the stories I've heard from different saints I've known. They shared these stories with me with bright eyes and firm conviction, telling me of the ways You came through for them. Your intervention might not have been significant to anyone else, but to them it was the answer and power they needed.

All Your children can trust in You, knowing You will work on their behalf. Sometimes You choose to deliver; and sometimes You choose to walk with us in the midst of our fiery trials, as You did with the Hebrew men in the furnace. But in everything we encounter, You are our salvation and stronghold. I praise Your name today! Amen.

ON THE THRONE

I will praise You, O LORD, with my whole heart; I will tell of all Your marvelous works. I will be glad and rejoice in You; I will sing praise to Your name, O Most High. When my enemies turn back, they shall fall and perish at Your presence. For You have maintained my right and my cause; You sat on the throne judging in righteousness. You have rebuked the nations, You have destroyed the wicked; You have blotted out their name forever and ever.

PSALM 9:1–5 NKJV

Lord God, I am comforted today to know that You are on the throne and ruling over the affairs of the universe. If a mere man were in charge of things, what a mess everything would be! But You, Lord, rule in justice and righteousness. The kingdoms of this world may rise to the top for a time; but when they refuse to acknowledge You, they crumble. The ruins of great world civilizations still exist—Egypt, Babylon, Rome, Aztec, and Maya—and they stand as shabby sentinels to tell us that those who rise too high in their own opinion will fall.

Today and forever, You are on the throne. I trust in You and praise You for who You are. Amen.

FULL OF HIS GOODNESS

Rejoice in the LORD, O you righteous! For praise from the upright is beautiful. Praise the LORD with the harp; make melody to Him with an instrument of ten strings. Sing to Him a new song; play skillfully with a shout of joy. For the word of the LORD is right, and all His work is done in truth. He loves righteousness and justice; the earth is full of the goodness of the LORD.

PSALM 33:1–5 NKJV

. . . .

Lord God Almighty, You are Maker of heaven and earth. You are the divine cadence of all life. You bring forth every good thing in heaven above and on the earth below. Today I read these words of praise to You and respond with my heart. No orchestra on earth can adequately render an anthem of praise to tell of Your greatness.

The story is told that the audience stood up in awe when the "Hallelujah Chorus" composed by George Frideric Handel was first played. And Handel himself felt that he was inspired to try to display the splendor of scripture in his *Messiah*. But that is only a dim earthly tune compared to the majestic strains of heaven that praise You. I look forward to hearing the melodies someday. Amen.

EXALTED ABOVE ALL

Sing praises to God, sing praises! Sing praises to our King, sing praises! For God is the King of all the earth; sing praises with understanding. God reigns over the nations; God sits on His holy throne. The princes of the people have gathered together, the people of the God of Abraham. For the shields of the earth belong to God; He is greatly exalted.

PSALM 47:6–9 NKJV

Lord God, today's verses tell me to sing. You gave me the voice I have to praise You. I was made to communicate with You and with others. And You hear not only my actual speaking voice and singing voice, but also my heart. I can talk to You and praise You while in a crowd of people or in a setting of absolute silence. But how much better it is for me to let my voice ring out and be heard! With all believers past and present, I bow in Your presence and bring my praise to You. You are highly exalted in the earth and in my heart! Amen.

AWESOME WORKS

Come and see the works of God; He is awesome in
His doing toward the sons of men. He turned the sea
into dry land; they went through the river on foot.
There we will rejoice in Him. He rules by His power
forever; His eyes observe the nations; do not let the
rebellious exalt themselves. Oh, bless our God, you
peoples! And make the voice of His praise to be heard.

PSALM 66:5–8 NKJV

Dear Father, one of the greatest demonstrations of Your power was the parting of the Red Sea long ago. You delivered Your people from the hand of Pharaoh and led them out of captivity. But soon they faced the impossible situation of the sea on one hand and Pharaoh's army on the other. There was no way out. But You are never stymied by earthly situations. You simply made a way through the sea and brought them through to the other side. And then You did it again with the river Jordan! There is no end to Your awesome works, and today I need to remember that truth as I go about my day.

Before long, I will face some impossibility and need the encouragement these stories provide. I praise You for being the same through every generation. Amen.

DWELLING AND POSSESSING

Let Your salvation, O God, set me up on high. I will praise the name of God with a song, and will magnify Him with thanksgiving. . . . Let heaven and earth praise Him, the seas and everything that moves in them. For God will save Zion and build the cities of Judah, that they may dwell there and possess it. Also, the descendants of His servants shall inherit it, and those who love His name shall dwell in it.

PSALM 69:29–30, 34–36 NKJV

. . . .

Lord, You own all things, as shown in this verse that says the seas and everything in them are Yours. We humans put great stock in ownership. We spend our working years trying to buy houses and property and accumulate enough savings so that we can retire and enjoy several years of ease and comfort. And You don't condemn this plan if it includes generosity to others and a recognition that it all belongs to You. But I want to remember that You actually own all the earth; You may lend it to us for a while, but the deed is still in Your name. You are Creator and Sustainer. Thank You for Your generous provision! Amen.

ALL DAY LONG

*You, who have shown me great and severe troubles,
shall revive me again, and bring me up again from the
depths of the earth. You shall increase my greatness,
and comfort me on every side. Also with the lute I
will praise You—and Your faithfulness, O my God! To
You I will sing with the harp, O Holy One of Israel.
My lips shall greatly rejoice when I sing to You, and
my soul, which You have redeemed. My tongue also
shall talk of Your righteousness all the day long.*

PSALM 71:20-24 NKJV

Father in heaven, as I go through my week, help me to
remember to spend time in prayer and praise. I praise You
for my blessings and bring my troubles and concerns to
You. When I have a heart of praise, the things I need don't
bother me as much as they do when I focus on myself. I
will voice my praise by telling someone else what You've
done for me in the past. And I will believe that You will
continue to meet all my needs in the future. Amen.

CONTINUAL PRAISE

Let the heavens praise your wonders, O LORD,
your faithfulness in the assembly of the holy ones!
For who in the skies can be compared to the LORD?
Who among the heavenly beings is like the LORD,
a God greatly to be feared in the council of the holy
ones, and awesome above all who are around him?
O LORD God of hosts, who is mighty as you are,
O LORD, with your faithfulness all around you?

PSALM 89:5–8 ESV

Lord God, praise is the anthem of heaven. Continual praise ascends to You as the hosts of heaven murmur Your greatness. They herald Your holiness and declare Your majesty. When Jesus rode into Jerusalem long ago and the religious leaders were upset with the chanting crowds, He told them that the very stones would cry out in praise if the people were silent! There must be praise to You! I want to praise You willingly and exuberantly now and for eternity. No one compares to You, Lord. I celebrate Your faithfulness and goodness. Amen.

EVERLASTING MERCY

Make a joyful noise unto the LORD, all ye lands.
Serve the LORD with gladness: come before his
presence with singing. Know ye that the LORD he
is God: it is he that hath made us, and not we
ourselves; we are his people, and the sheep of his
pasture. Enter into his gates with thanksgiving,
and into his courts with praise: be thankful unto him,
and bless his name. For the LORD is good; his mercy is
everlasting; and his truth endureth to all generations.

PSALM 100 KJV

Dear Lord, the words of this psalm are so familiar, yet they speak great truth. You are good. Everything You do is good. We are Your people, and You work in us for good. We can enter into Your gates with thankful hearts and bless Your name. In biblical times, there were limits to where the people could go in the temple. But now, through Christ, we have complete access to You. We can come into Your presence with our heartfelt praise. Thank You for Your everlasting mercy and truth. I want to live in them all my days. Amen.

OPENED EYES

Blessed are you, O LORD; teach me your statutes!
With my lips I declare all the rules of your mouth. In
the way of your testimonies I delight as much as in all
riches. I will meditate on your precepts and fix my eyes
on your ways. I will delight in your statutes; I will not
forget your word. Deal bountifully with your servant,
that I may live and keep your word. Open my eyes,
that I may behold wondrous things out of your law.

PSALM 119:12–18 ESV

Heavenly Father, You created my earthly eyes. When I was being formed in my mother's womb, You fashioned my eye sockets and caused my eyeballs to take shape. You knew the color they would be long before I ever took a breath. You have given me the gift of earthly sight. But You have also given me the gift of spiritual sight since I came to faith in You. You have enabled me to see truths and principles that I couldn't discern before I knew You. Today I ask You to open my spiritual eyes again so that I can understand how great You truly are. When I fix my heart and eyes on Your ways, I am amazed and encouraged in You. Amen.

PRAISE FROM NATURE

*Praise the LORD! Praise the LORD from the
heavens; praise him in the heights! Praise him,
all his angels; praise him, all his hosts! Praise him,
sun and moon, praise him, all you shining stars!
Praise him, you highest heavens, and you waters above
the heavens! . . . Praise the LORD from the earth, you
great sea creatures and all deeps, fire and hail, snow
and mist, stormy wind fulfilling his word! . . . Let them
praise the name of the LORD, for his name alone is
exalted; his majesty is above earth and heaven.*

PSALM 148:1–4, 7–8, 13 ESV

. . . .

Creator God, nature does what You created it to do. And
in doing so, it brings glory to You. When the sea creatures
romp and play, when the great whales breach, when the
snow falls and the mist rises, when the storms roll in and
the sun and moon come out of their hiding places, You
are glorified. Thank You for Your astounding creation. I
want to join all nature in praising You! Amen.

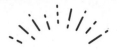

JOIN THE CELEBRATION

*Praise the L*ORD*! Praise God in his sanctuary; praise him in his mighty heavens! Praise him for his mighty deeds; praise him according to his excellent greatness! Praise him with trumpet sound; praise him with lute and harp! Praise him with tambourine and dance; praise him with strings and pipe! Praise him with sounding cymbals; praise him with loud clashing cymbals! Let everything that has breath praise the L*ORD*! Praise the L*ORD*!*

PSALM 150:1–6 ESV

Lord God of all, these verses tell me we should use what we have to praise You! Since I'm not an orchestra conductor, I don't have all these instruments at hand. But I do have some things I can offer:

- A schedule
- A mind
- A voice
- An attitude
- A twenty-four-hour day
- A smile
- A hug
- A life

Today I will use these gifts to give back to You by helping someone else. My offering of praise is lifted to You as I reach out to others. Amen.

THE HOLY ONE

"Behold, God is my salvation; I will trust, and will not be afraid; for the LORD GOD is my strength and my song, and he has become my salvation." . . . "Give thanks to the LORD, call upon his name, make known his deeds among the peoples, proclaim that his name is exalted. Sing praises to the LORD, for he has done gloriously; let this be made known in all the earth. Shout, and sing for joy, O inhabitant of Zion, for great in your midst is the Holy One of Israel."

ISAIAH 12:2, 4–6 ESV

Lord God, many of the praises in the Bible focus on Your work for Your people Israel. You chose them to be the earthly lineage through which You brought the Redeemer. And You made them Your covenant people in order to demonstrate Your power and righteousness to all the earth. Because of Christ, everyone is welcomed into Your family now, and we rejoice in that truth. But You will never forget Your covenant with Your beloved, and Your name will always be exalted in Zion.

Thank You, Lord, for making a place for me in Your great heritage. I bless Your name. Amen.

GOD OF MIDNIGHT EARTHQUAKES

About midnight Paul and Silas were praying and singing hymns to God, and the prisoners were listening to them, and suddenly there was a great earthquake, so that the foundations of the prison were shaken. And immediately all the doors were opened, and everyone's bonds were unfastened.

ACTS 16:25–26 ESV

Lord, so many sermons and songs have centered on this story from the New Testament. We can see in it exactly how powerful praise to You can be. It reminds us that in our dark hours, when everything has been stripped from us, our praise to You remains. We can praise You in prison; we can praise You in pain. We can praise You in suffering; we can praise You in grief. We can praise You in loneliness; we can praise You in chaos. We can praise You anytime, anywhere, because praise is a choice we make. We can even praise You in the quiet of our minds, and You will bless us when we do. Today, in my difficult moments, help me remember to praise You despite my circumstances. And when I do, remind me to look for earthquakes. Amen.

SACRIFICE OF PRAISE

For here we have no lasting city, but we seek
the city that is to come. Through him then let us
continually offer up a sacrifice of praise to God,
that is, the fruit of lips that acknowledge his name.
Do not neglect to do good and to share what you
have, for such sacrifices are pleasing to God.

HEBREWS 13:14–16 ESV

Heavenly Father, today I bring to You my praise for the city that is coming. I have lived in many places while on earth, but the best place I will ever live is in Your presence someday. You are preparing a city for me and for all the others who trust in You. I'm so grateful I don't have to worry about getting there; I don't have to figure out how to find it. You are taking care of all the details, and all I have to do is keep my faith in You.

While I live here on earth, I will do my best to share what I have, because consideration for others and generosity are sacrifices I can make to You. And they please You. Sacrifices are never easy, but they demonstrate what we value. I offer my life and my possessions to You. Amen.

PRAISE FOR SALVATION

In this you rejoice, though now for a little while, if necessary, you have been grieved by various trials, so that the tested genuineness of your faith—more precious than gold that perishes though it is tested by fire—may be found to result in praise and glory and honor at the revelation of Jesus Christ. Though you have not seen him, you love him. Though you do not now see him, you believe in him and rejoice with joy that is inexpressible and filled with glory, obtaining the outcome of your faith, the salvation of your souls.

1 PETER 1:6–9 ESV

Lord Jesus, I have never seen You with my physical eyes, but I look forward to that joy someday. I believe in You and love You by faith. But someday I will have supernatural sight. Right now my faith is often tested so that someday it may be as solid and pure as gold. The trials I endure keep me looking to You for strength and grace. I praise You because You have never failed me, and I know You never will! Amen.

PROCLAIMING HIS EXCELLENCIES

But you are a chosen race, a royal priesthood, a holy nation, a people for his own possession, that you may proclaim the excellencies of him who called you out of darkness into his marvelous light. Once you were not a people, but now you are God's people; once you had not received mercy, but now you have received mercy.... He himself bore our sins in his body on the tree, that we might die to sin and live to righteousness. By his wounds you have been healed. For you were straying like sheep, but have now returned to the Shepherd and Overseer of your souls.

1 PETER 2:9–10, 24–25 ESV

• •

Father God, I praise You today because I have been invited to be included in the people You call Your own. I praise You because You have called me out of darkness. I praise You because I have received mercy. I praise You because You bore my sins in Your own body on the cross. I praise You because I am healed by Your wounds. I praise You because You are the Shepherd of my soul. I praise You for my very life! Amen.

THE GREAT DAY

And from the throne came a voice saying, "Praise our God, all you his servants, you who fear him, small and great." . . . "Hallelujah! For the Lord our God the Almighty reigns. Let us rejoice and exult and give him the glory, for the marriage of the Lamb has come, and his Bride has made herself ready; it was granted her to clothe herself with fine linen, bright and pure"—for the fine linen is the righteous deeds of the saints.

REVELATION 19:5–8 ESV

Heavenly Father, as I come to this final prayer, I want to rejoice in anticipation of that great day when I will join all the others who love You and look forward to Your coming! I will rejoice with You forever in the place You have prepared for Your people. As part of the Bride of Christ, I am invited to that great marriage feast where joy and peace will reign and sin and sorrow will be no more. I will have new garments to wear and will never be parted from You. O Lord, I praise You and ask You to keep me in Your grace until I hear that final call. In the name of Him who died for me, I pray. Amen.

SCRIPTURE INDEX

THE OLD TESTAMENT

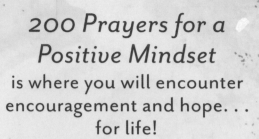

200 Prayers for a Positive Mindset is where you will encounter encouragement and hope. . . for life!

These 200 devotional-like prayers will encourage you to be mindful and pray as you encounter peace and hope for everyday living.

Each prayer begins with a relatable scripture selection to help clear your mind as you begin your one-on-one time in the heavenly Father's presence.

Whether you are overworked, overstressed, overwhelmed, or just "over" the craziness of life, you will welcome the peace and comfort this delightful prayer book brings to your daily quiet time.

A POSITIVE MINDSET IS JUST A PRAYER AWAY!

Religion / Christian Life / Prayer

U.S. $9.99

ISBN 978-1-63609-380-2

50999

9 781636 093802

BARBOUR
PUBLISHING